INSPIRATIONAL
JOURNEYS
AWAKENING THE SOUL

Ramona Crabtree-Falkner

Table of Contents

Forward

Authentic. Magical. Adventurer. These are just a few of many words I could use to describe Ramona, and after reading this book you will know why.

She's, a seeker, a guide, and the embodiment of the goddess.

I have walked the path toward my own transformation with Ramona as my guide, so when she told me she was writing a book I knew firsthand that it was going to be magical.

It's an invitation for us to journey with her: from her profound spiritual encounter following a traumatic event that shook her to her core, to friendships lost and found, to magical moments in the mountains and in the ocean, and everything in between.

Ramona taught me how to manifest my dreams and claim my soul's purpose. May this book be a guide to your own soul's awakening.

Trust the process. Trust yourself.

Your divine purpose awaits!

Paige Friend

Co-Creator, Invoking the Divine Goddess

Introduction

This book is much more than a compendium of short stories and chapters. It is an expedition into the depths of human transformation, spiritual enlightenment, and self-discovery. It is for everyone who has ever sensed a stirring within, for people who have endured difficulties and are looking for growth and purpose from them, and for anybody who is looking for love, light, and a closer connection to who they truly are.

Who Is This Book For?

- The Seekers: If you find yourself searching for more — more depth, more meaning, more understanding of yourself and the world around you — this book is for you.
- The Healing Hearts: For those who are on a journey of healing, whether from loss, trauma, or the daily struggles of life, these pages offer companionship and insights into the healing process.
- The Dreamers and Doers: If you aspire to live a life aligned with your deepest dreams and values, this book offers both inspiration and practical steps to guide you on your path.

Read in an interactive way

Approach the book not just as a reader but as an active participant. As you journey through each chapter, immerse yourself in the narratives, allowing them to resonate with your own life experiences. Keep a journal close at hand to capture your thoughts, emotions, and any epiphanies that surface. This practice turns reading into a dialogue between you and the book, making each story a reflection of your own journey.

Take a break between chapters

After you complete a chapter, give yourself a moment to absorb its essence. Reflect on the lessons and insights, and engage with any reflective questions or exercises provided. These pauses are crucial as they allow you to connect more deeply with the material, letting it simmer in your mind and heart. Think of these moments as checkpoints where you align the book's wisdom with your own life path.

Respect your rhythm

There's no rush to finish this book. Your reading journey should align with your personal pace. Some chapters might prompt you to linger, while others might energize you to move forward more quickly. Respect this rhythm; it's a part of the unique way you connect with the book's content. This book is a journey meant to be savored, not a destination to be hurriedly reached.

Sharing is caring

This book can be a powerful tool for connection. Share your insights and experiences from the book with friends, family, or even a book club. These discussions can open up new perspectives and deepen your understanding of the book's teachings. Sharing your journey adds a communal dimension to your experience, enriching it with diverse viewpoints and insights.

Apply the lessons to your life

As you progress through your reading, look for opportunities to integrate its lessons into your daily life. Whether it's adopting a new perspective on challenges or practicing gratitude, strive to embody the teachings of the book. Applying these insights transforms them from abstract concepts to tangible, life-changing practices.

Read... and read again!

My goal with this book is to make it a lifelong travel buddy. Please do not hesitate to peruse its pages again in times of need of motivation, support, or community. Every time you go back, you will gain fresh perspectives and understandings that will mirror the continuous process of your own development.

This is a reflection of the common journey of transformation, not simply my narrative. It is an invitation for you to bravely, honestly, and with a sense of adventure pursue your path. I hope this book is a constant companion on your journey to soul-awakening.

Happy reading!

Chapter 1

First Contact With The Divine

The healing journey is not linear; it's more closely related to a spiraling staircase. When one begins to awaken to the soul's call for healing, growth, and expansion, it is quite often experienced as chaos and intense upheaval. For me this was true. I had to fall apart to come back together and embrace my true purpose—to share my light with others.

My first experience with a spiritual encounter occurred at 24 years old, my senior year of college. I had big plans for the coming year and spent the summer bartending at a pool hall to make extra money to support my dream of living off campus that year. I had friends I worked with that I found happiness being with and a manager who was a joyful being and brought that light to us daily. He was a friend and I was so grateful to know him.

One fateful night just days before my senior year was to begin, we were working together and all was as it always was— a chill night at the pool hall until it wasn't. Within a split second, your life can change and this night was one of those nights. I remember sitting on a box behind the bar chatting with my boss when suddenly someone jumped up on the bar. I was shuffled into the office located behind the bar, where my boss was sitting.

It took me a moment to understand what was happening. Once the gun was in my face I was snapped into the clear understanding that we were being robbed. I stared in disbelief at the barrel of the gun. I saw the eyes of the gunman peering back at me just beyond the barrel. He yelled to not look at him, so I looked down in great fear. Suddenly my boss's hand is on my shoulder and I feel him guiding me to crouch down.

Once I was crouched down, I placed my hands over my head. I am terrified. I hear the gunman yelling and my boss yelling back "Take it, take it all". I see money being flung out of the safe. I close my eyes and I'm blank. I'm in disbelief that this is really happening. I feel like I'm dreaming. Suddenly, I hear a gunshot followed by a loud ringing sound. I flinch and am overcome with emotions. I thought for certain that my life was over.

The room became very quiet and all the commotion seemed to stop. It was as if I was frozen and couldn't remember how to move. Timidly, I began to pull my hands from my head and look around noticing that the gunman was gone. I placed my hand on my boss's back and called out to him several times. He does not respond and I have no idea why until he falls forward and blood begins to pour out onto the floor. I begin to cry out. I jumped up and ran to lock the door out of fear that the robbers were still there.

I pick up the phone and call 911. I'm scared and realize my boss is dead. I begin to cry as I'm speaking to the police doing my best to explain what had happened. They reassure me that someone's on the way to help. All I can do is slide down the door sobbing—frightened and disillusioned.

Then someone knocks on the door and I begin to scream out fearful the robbers have returned. The person on the other side of the door announces who they are, a customer that I know, and I slowly open the door. I walk out of the office and run to the front door to lock us in. I walked around the pool hall to see if anyone else was hurt and no one was physically injured.

I walked around the building questioning every step I took. How I am here, how did this happen, what do I do, and how am I still alive? The process of a homicide investigation is long and requires many questions that go on until the early morning hours. I'm exhausted by the time they tell me I can go home. Once home my parents are called and I'm numb. Within days I was on a flight home to see my family.

I stay in Florida for a weekend and have to decide if I will return to finish my final year of college. My parents are grateful to see me and hold me and I'm still numb. I find it difficult to reconcile the whole experience I'm having. After a few days, I decided that I needed to finish my senior year and go back. This will require some changes in my plans for housing. I would have to contact the school to see about returning to the dorms, as living alone off campus is no longer an option I wanted to take.

Luckily, there is one space left open in the girl's dorm and I take it. Once I arrive, I get checked into my dorm and meet my new roommate (a foreign exchange student from Japan). This turned out to be the best thing for me at this moment in my life. She was a very gentle and easeful person which is exactly what I needed.

In the following days, weeks, and months I had to begin therapy. I also had to continue to be a college student and still had to answer questions from the police. It was a very dark time in my life. Looking back, I felt very alone at this time in my life. I was getting by each day but also felt overwhelmed and lost. During this dark time, I first experienced spirit speaking to me.

Within the first few weeks after the robbery and after returning to school, my dreams were very active. I would dream about all kinds of things including reliving the night over and over. One night the dream was different. Most times in my dreams I would see it as it happened from my vantage point. This night the dream was from a viewpoint that was outside of myself.

In the dream, I was looking down at myself from the far corner of the room. I didn't even see anyone else. I only saw myself crouched down in the opposite corner. As I saw myself, I suddenly saw a vision of Angel's wings wrapping around my whole body to the point that I could no longer see myself. All I could see were the wings crossing over each other creating a safe place for me to be while this tragic event happened.

I woke up and my mind was racing. What was that? I did my best to recall the vision I saw in the dream. I wanted to hold it close to my heart and remember this. I don't know why I felt so called to remember this image, almost like I needed to. I kept this image and this dream to myself for some time. It wasn't until my sister came in early for my graduation that I finally shared this dream with her.

Since this time I have reflected and recalled this dream many times. I now recognize it was the first time I experienced the Divine (angels, spirit, spiritual guides, or god/goddess) making its presence known to me. I don't know that I can say I had this awareness at that moment. However, today where I am in my life and spiritual journey I know it was the Divine helping me remember and show me I am not alone.

It was also a foreshadowing of my life today and the work I am gifted to share with others. I know in my heart it was the Divine showing me I had more to do in this life. I also recognize the gift my boss was in my life for more reasons than just being my friend. He was my protector that night—a human angel. I live every day in gratitude for his hand gently guiding me to crouch down so I would be protected that night. I honor him every year we return to the date of this fateful night.

It took many more years before I was truly awake to the knowledge of the Divine but once the spark of awakening began that night everything was put into motion. There were still many years of suffering I experienced before finding myself in awareness of the spiritual journey I was on. I was still being guided and nudged along the way until I was truly ready to wake up and step into my soul's purpose.

Reflection: Traumatic experiences can serve as a catalyst for profound spiritual awakening. Embracing our most challenging moments often leads us to discover inner strength and resilience we never knew we had.

Even though traumatic events are very hard, they often serve as turning points in our lives that lead us in surprising directions of deep personal growth and spiritual awakening. Even though they are painful, these events can uncover deeper parts of our lives that make us face who we are and what is important in life. When we are going through hard times, we often have to ask ourselves deep questions about our purpose, our strength, and our ability to change and heal. When we really think about ourselves, we start to find parts of ourselves that we had forgotten about because of our old habits and ways of thinking.

Let us use a source of inner strength and resilience that we have not used before as we get through these rough times. It is like finding a secret, strong, and peaceful place inside yourself that has been waiting to give you comfort and wisdom. Finding comfort in ourselves is not the only reason we turn inward; it is also a journey of change that makes us question our values, beliefs, and even our very selves. Sometimes we have to work hard to learn these lessons, but they give us a new appreciation for life, a deeper knowledge of other people's struggles, and a better sense of our own path.

Also, traumatic events can sometimes break down the walls that keep us from reaching a higher spiritual knowledge. A lot of people find spiritual insights and links that give them a sense of peace, purpose, and connection as they look for meaning in a wild world. This spiritual awakening is very personal and changes us. It gives us a new way to see the world and our place in it. It is like the trials have taken away the fog, letting us see the world and ourselves more clearly and deeply.

When we accept these hard times, we do not just get over them; we come out of them renewed, with a better knowledge of life and a stronger sense of who we are. This journey is not easy, and there are times when I question myself and feel hopeless. But the strength we build and the knowledge we gain become part of who we are and help us face future obstacles with grace and strength. When we let our worst experiences teach us the most, they can lead to an awakening that brings us closer to our real selves and our potential for growth and happiness.

Chapter 2

The Journey to Healing

In the years after the robbery I continued aimlessly through life. I moved from one moment to the next just pushing forward through life. This was a trait I had developed over my lifetime to just keep on keeping on. I know now this was a response to trauma, to want to escape the terrible thing I experienced, and keeping busy and constantly moving was my way of avoiding the fears that lived within me every day.

At 28 years old I had my son and this time gave me an opportunity to decide how I wanted to move forward with my work-life balance. I decided to pursue my dream of becoming a massage therapist instead of returning to my job as an audio-visual exhibit sales representative. This was the beginning of the journey that I now have found myself upon. I chose to return home and attend school in Florida, where I gained the support of my mother and family to help with my son. When I entered this training, I had no idea where this choice would take me. I am grateful that I listened to the little nudge inside me to take the leap of faith and go for it.

Looking back upon this one decision, I am in awe. In hindsight, I can see that the Divine has been working through me all along. Waking up to the Divine is a process especially when you have been so conditioned to believe that you are alone and all the decisions are of your own making. I see now that I was being nudged along every step of the way even in the times I was unaware of Spirit's presence.

Once I finished massage school, I took the test to practice and we officially moved to Florida. So many more things would happen before I was really awakened to the healing journey. Over the many years of continued aimless living, I felt like a victim in my life. Every corner of my life seemed like one difficulty after another. All of the suffering was of my own making but I didn't really see it that way. The victim mentality was strong and I was rigid in my thoughts and expectations. This is when yoga became the next important choice I made.

I had practiced yoga since before my son was born. My college best friend, Jody, shared yoga with me in her home. After my son was born, Wednesday night yoga and dinner became our ritual until I left for massage school. Once I came back to Florida for school, I was eager to find a place to attend yoga. At that time yoga was not as widely known and taught as it is now. I had a difficult time finding a place that offered yoga and eventually, I gave up the practice. Until I had found a place to teach yoga, a local gym I attended offered me the opportunity and the owner didn't require training for me to teach. I felt a natural calling to teach yoga as it was such an amazing tool in my life I wanted more than anything to share it with others. I was nervous but I just taught what I knew and that was just the spark I needed. A few years later I was supported by my dad to open my own massage business. I knew I wanted yoga to be a part of the business and I sought out yoga teacher training. Over 5 years, I took one course a week or weekend a year and taught in tandem with this training within my business.

At first, I thought yoga was simply a physical body exercise. Ultimately, what I ended up learning was that yoga is a philosophy to live by. It was the gateway to connect me to spirit and to truly learn to know who I am—physically, mentally, emotionally, and spiritually. The training weeks or weekends were intense and required a great deal of focus and effort. At this same time, I'm running a business, working 7 days a week, and caring for my son as a single mother. I felt under the weeds nearly every day, still pushing forward with old paradigms of belief. This forceful way of living would eventually catch up to me and my physical body would show the signs of disease.

I had spent so many years collecting knowledge and applying that knowledge to the work I did but I wasn't really living what I was learning. My ego was strong and kept me in a place of suffering and force. These were some of the darkest of days. I have had a very dense emotional body throughout my life. I didn't really understand what this meant until I opened my heart and eyes and began to live the healing modalities I had been learning. This became the cornerstone of my teachings today— to live and integrate the teachings and not just collect them to give to others.

This understanding wouldn't fully come to my awareness until I fell completely apart. Chaos had to happen for me to wake up fully. For me, it was a long journey of deconstructing before I could hear the voice of the Divine clearly. I was always nudged along and connected in a superficial way to my divinity. It wasn't until I was drowning that I was ready and willing to do the work. The work that was necessary for me to truly begin to co-create with the Divine. I had to recognize and accept that it was not me, my personality, that was creating it. It was the Divine working through me.

Insight: Healing is a personal journey that often requires us to break free from our past patterns and embrace new paths, even if they initially seem daunting or unfamiliar.

Healing is a very personal process that takes a different shape and time for each person. It often means giving up long-held views, habits, and ways of acting that are not good for our growth or well-being. This departure is important, but it can be scary. In order to heal and grow, it asks us to leave the safety of known miseries and step into the unknown. It takes courage to go on this trip because we have to face and let go of parts of our past that have shaped who we are and how we see the world.

Breaking out of these patterns is like finding your way through a complicated maze. At each turn, you have a choice: to go back to old habits or to keep going toward new opportunities. It takes work to see these trends for what they are and how they affect our lives. These habits have often been our defenses, our ways of dealing with the hard things in life. Letting go of them means coming up with new, healthier, and more productive ways to deal with these problems. Unlearning and relearning is an important part of healing. It means being aware of where our behaviors come from and what sets them off, and then picking a different response every time they happen.

Taking on new routes as part of your healing process is more than just picking different things. Transforming the story we tell ourselves about who we are and what we can do is what it is all about. It means changing negative thoughts about yourself and criticism with kindness and support, understanding that healing is a process that has ups and downs instead of a straight line. It is about learning to be kind to ourselves and understand that each small step forward is a win in and of itself.

In the end, the path to healing is a path to change. It is about finding ourselves again, maybe even parts of ourselves we did not know we had. We can learn more about our strengths, weaknesses, and ability to change as we go on this trip. There are challenges along this path, but there are also chances to grow as a person and find a new sense of purpose and satisfaction. When we accept this trip, we open ourselves up to a life where we do not just survive, but thrive in our truest selves.

Chapter 3

It's Time to Wake Up!

In 2015 my body was screaming for me to get help. The year prior I spent training for and completing a Half Ironman race. This experience taught me a lot. Once I was done, I put it all down and found I was not well. Over the following year, I had to pause everything and focus on my body.

In 2011 I was sitting and chatting with my sister when I noticed something odd under my chin, it seemed I had some kind of growth, and reached out to an ENT to have it checked out. Once my appointment came up I was evaluated and it was decided that I would need to get a CAT scan to confirm what was going on. On Christmas Eve the doctor's office called me so the doctor could speak to me. He told me that the growth was a cyst and was nothing to be concerned with but that they found something on my Thyroid Gland and that I needed to have further testing to determine what next steps would have to be taken. The next month of my life was long and stressful until I was able to get further testing.

In mid-January 2012, the testing had finally been completed, and I returned to the doctor's office to receive the news. When the doctor came in he brought with him a second doctor and discussed the need to have surgery and to be referred to an endocrinologist for further evaluation before surgery. Once I saw the endocrinologist it was determined that surgery would be the best path to take. Little did I know what this decision would create, years of difficulty in finding balance.

After the surgery, I dealt with difficulty finding balance with my thyroid levels and couldn't quite find the right doctors at that point to help me reach balance. In addition, I was experiencing a great deal of pain in my lower back and legs, as well as chronic inflammation. All of this had me focused on Western medicine as the answer. Little did I know my whole life was about to change again.

In the Fall of 2015, I was exposed to a video about the power of thought and how the energy of thought can heal the body. This video inspired and woke me up to a deeper understanding of healing through mind, body, and spirit practices such as energy work, mindfulness, breathwork, and eastern body care. I knew about this work because I had been a practitioner in the field of yoga & massage for 9 years and was sharing many of the modalities with others throughout that time. The funny thing about being a wellness practitioner is sometimes we don't always practice what we do. I had been receiving healing sessions from practitioners to a point but I don't know that I can say I was really living what I had learned.

After the exposure to the video, I was still focused on getting healed through Western medicine as I hadn't quite gotten the message just yet. All of this was about to change. That little spark of inspiration was the first key to awakening my soul's call to remember who I really was and begin the journey home, to my true self.

The year was coming to an end and I was still dealing with pain and discomfort in so many ways in my body. I was getting shots, getting scans & X-rays, taking medications, and doing anything that the doctors told me to do, and still, my pain didn't seem to be getting better. I was feeling tremendously frustrated and uncertain about what to do. One day a thought popped into my head to reach out to a friend of mine who is an acupuncturist so I immediately called and scheduled an appointment. After the first session, I felt relief and for the first time all year experienced hope.

While still continuing with all my doctors, I saw her for more sessions weekly until we couldn't meet for one week due to a holiday week. This was an illuminating week because I had spent a few weeks feeling hopeful. When I didn't see her for a week, my pain came screaming back and I found myself once again fearful I was never going to find true relief. I scheduled my next appointment as soon as I could get in after the holiday but still had to wait.

I woke up on December 1st and had a nudge from within to find the video I had been exposed to just months before and watch it again. So I searched for the video and found a different version of the same talk and this one had even more information to inspire me. As I sat and observed this speaker I felt within me a knowing that I had to shift my direction and take a different path for my healing.

Immediately I began to formulate a plan to bring together all I know how to do and find ways to give these modalities to myself or find someone to care for me. I was inspired and my soul began to sing a song, sharing every possible way I could apply what I needed to do to find healing.

What I could do for myself I began that day, with yoga, breathing, meditation, visualization, Pilates & Reiki. Next, I began to seek out practitioners and friends who could help or guide me to the right resources and I set up sessions. Little by little over the month of December I began to feel better and I ended my Western medicine treatment plan.

During this time, I kept hearing 6 months and I wasn't really sure what that meant. Looking back now I can tell you that within 6 months everything changed. Not only had I found more ease and comfort in my body I also began seeing a vision of what was to come with my work. The groundwork began to be laid and I was on the path to healing for my mind, body, and spirit.

Takeaway: Our bodies often communicate what our minds try to ignore. Listening to and honoring our physical and emotional signals can guide us toward necessary changes and healing.

Our bodies are amazing messengers; they frequently convey to us subtle—and occasionally not so subtle—signals about our general state of health. These warnings can take many forms, such as ongoing exhaustion, physical discomfort, emotional swings, or even unexplained changes in our health. Sadly, it is all too simple to ignore these signals in the midst of everyday chaos and chalk them up to stress or life's inevitable abrasions. These physical indicators, however, are frequently our inner selves attempting to convey important details about our desires, anxieties, and unsolved problems.

Healing and personal development require us to learn how to understand and interpret these signals from our bodies. It calls for developing an attitude of mindfulness and awareness, tuning in to our emotional and physical states with an open mind and no bias. For example, recurrent headaches may indicate not only physical strain but also unresolved stress or emotional burden. Similar to this, persistent tiredness may be the body's way of telling you that you need to take care of yourself—possibly intellectually and emotionally as well as physically.

Respecting these cues entails proactively addressing them. It could be getting medical advice, making lifestyle changes, participating in therapeutic activities, or just giving ourselves permission to take time off and heal. Additionally, this approach frequently highlights underlying problems that we may have been denying or repressing. A vital step in the healing process is addressing these underlying problems. It is important to identify and address the underlying reasons for our suffering rather than merely addressing its symptoms.

More broadly, listening to our bodies promotes a healthy connection between our mental and emotional as well as our physical selves. It encourages an all-encompassing perspective on health and wellness, viewing the body, mind, and spirit as interdependent and interrelated. Beginning to pay attention to the signals coming from our bodies sets us on a path of self-healing and self-discovery that can result in a more harmonious, healthy, and satisfying life. Relearning the language of our bodies and reacting to them with respect and care is the goal of this journey. It acknowledges that genuine healing and well-being are holistic processes that touch on all facets of our existence.

Chapter 4

Six Months to Toronto

I can honestly say I have had a very rigid mind and still today, I have to work the edges of that rigidness. The next six months I begin the journey of softening my mind and opening my heart. Opening my heart was truly the healing I was in need of because my mind had become so rigid that I couldn't see beyond the moment and I felt stuck all the time. This stuck feeling was what ultimately held me hostage to pain & suffering—physically, mentally, and emotionally. The process of getting unstuck wasn't easy, but it was necessary.

I began to find my way to listening to my soul's messages more as I began to quiet my mind. This started with meditation, which opened my intuition and allowed the divine spark from my heart to be heard. I attended weekly meditation classes and eventually found myself hearing ideas and inspiration as I was driving to my class. Of course, I couldn't write anything down, and I remember thinking "Really? Now is when you want to give me this information?" I had to figure something out, so I began to voice dictate every thought I had as I was driving because I knew if I didn't grab the ideas at the moment, they would be gone.

Within the first month of the year 2016, I dictated a program I was to create. Over the following month, I would sit to write and organize the program that ultimately became my next service for my business, mindfulness coaching, and the blueprint to my deeper healing and connection to the Divine.

In addition to following the flow of inspiration, I felt called to take a trip to a convention being held in Toronto to see and receive messages to open my heart even more from multiple speakers including the person who woke me up with their video the previous year reminding me of the power of energy healing and how I needed to apply what I do to my own healing.

It took very little effort for me to want to attend this convention yet I was nervous. This nervousness was rooted in so many things that I needed to give time and space to honor and understand so I could take this leap of faith and go for it. So began the journey of allowing myself to do something for myself that I yearned for but always felt was just out of my reach, to travel.

My 20s and 30s felt difficult and riddled with a mindset of lack. I spent so much time believing I couldn't do or have something because I couldn't afford it. I spent so much time in fear of money because I was a single mom or because I had to pay off debt or I got married and I couldn't do things for all kinds of reasons. That rigid mind ultimately found my body screaming at me. This is what showed up as I began to contemplate how I could do this and make this work.

As I meditated on going to the convention in Toronto my whole body lit up with YES, but still, I couldn't commit. I began to journal and self-explore why I was afraid, for that's what this was, fear. Once I began to honor the fear and commune with it, I began to find the answers and the fear began to fall away. Instead, I started to feel safer to make this decision and commit.

After several weeks I finally opened up the link, purchased my ticket, and searched for a plane ticket and a hotel. Suddenly it was done. I was going to Toronto. Now I just had to wait till May!

As April approached, I began to test-run my coaching program in small groups, flushing out the edges and finding more and more inspiration. As I experienced this process I felt called to open my heart to not only transforming my business but actually starting a whole new business.

The business would have similar elements to my original yoga & massage company, but my heart was showing me this new vision had its own purpose, Dharma, and needed to be planted and rooted as its own independent energy.

Lesson: Personal growth often involves stepping out of our comfort zones and embracing opportunities that align with our deeper passions and interests.

Moving out of our comfort zones is often necessary for personal growth because it is an ever-changing and difficult journey. Even though these zones are safe and comfortable, they can also stop us from growing by narrowing our experiences and not letting us reach our full potential. When we decide to push these limits and face the risks and unknowns that come with trying new things, going down roads, we have not been on before, and following our passions, we often start to grow.

Getting out of our comfort zones is not just about big jumps into the unknown; it is also about making small, everyday decisions that make us think and act in ways that are different from what we usually do. As an example, we could start a new hobby that interests us, speak up when we normally wouldn't, or set intentions that both scare and excite us. Even though these things may not seem important, they are all important steps toward broadening our horizons and finding parts of ourselves we did not know before.

An important part of this journey is taking advantage of chances that match our deeper interests and passions. Being self-aware and honest about what matters to us, not what we think should matter, is important. This alignment is not always clear-cut, and we may need to explore, try new things, and even reevaluate our values and goals from time to time. It can be uncomfortable because we have to question our own beliefs, face our fears, and sometimes deal with doubt or criticism from other people.

But the benefits of being so brave are immeasurable. When we leave our comfort zones, our lives become fuller, more interesting, and full of personal happiness and fulfillment. It helps us learn more about who we are, what we can do, and what gives our lives real joy and purpose. Personal growth is a process that never ends. What keeps this journey exciting and life-changing is the courage to leave our comfort zones. To live a fuller, more real life, we need to keep growing and stepping outside of our comfort zones, not just once, but all the time.

Chapter 5

A New Beginning

May had finally arrived, and I was about to leave for the convention. Traveling to another country alone to finally see and hear some of my favorite speakers and feel the vibrations of being in a room of like-minded people awakening to our soul's calling was invigorating. It was so exciting and I was filled with nervousness and anticipation!

The 5 days of this journey were transformative in so many ways. I met so many people, solo traveled, and took adventures in addition to taking in the inspiration of the speakers. It seemed like magic to be here and I knew I was exactly where I was supposed to be!

When I returned home, my view of the world and my life was anew. I was excited to continue to create a new vision for my work and was feeling inspired to share it with the world.

As I was reintegrating into life, I was allowing all I heard and experienced to unfold and open me up more. As I was journaling one day, I heard a clear message: "Authentic Life Journey." I wrote this down and thought, "What does that mean to me?"

I really wasn't sure at first what this message was but it was a clear message. I had been learning over the previous 6 months, that when I have a message that clearly comes through like this it is spirit speaking to me. All the meditation and healing I had been doing was allowing me to actually hear my intuition. I had been learning to trust those thoughts, feelings, and knowings because the more I followed these nudges, the more grounded and safe I felt and the more ease I had in my physical body.

As I sat with the message I asked myself many questions and the answers that arose in me all pointed to the same query, "Do you feel you are living an authentic life journey?" Wow, did I? The answer I came to was: NO.

Ouch, that hurt! I didn't feel I was living my authentic life and I had a lot of feelings about that. The initial feelings were rooted in judgment and self-abuse. Then I heard a small voice inside me say, "Please be gentle with yourself. I love you exactly as and where you are." This small voice that has been drowned out for so many years by my ego was finally being heard.

My heart was singing and was in the joy of my awakening to her voice. My spark of the Divine was finally being heard. This was when I felt I really began to see and understand why my body was screaming so loudly because it's my greatest messenger when I can't hear my soul's call. The more I began to open up to my healing, the more I understood the connection of my whole being—mind, body, and spirit.

This is the authentic life journey; remembering and then actively creating a life that honors my whole being. I am a physical body, a mental body, an emotional body, and a spiritual body. I am all of this and more. Aligning with this understanding became the next key to my soul purpose awakening. This is also when I realized the new beginning, my life, and my life's work is Authentic Life Journey!

Reflection: Realizing and stepping into our authentic selves can be a transformative experience, leading us to redefine our life's purpose and direction.

Realizing and stepping into our true selves is a path that changes us in ways that go beyond just finding out about ourselves. It is about getting to the heart of who we really are by peeling back the layers of expectations, social norms, and self-imposed limits. An important part of this journey is often taking time to think about our views, values, and what makes us who we are. For many of us, the noise of daily life drowns out our inner voice, that still, quiet voice that leads us to our real desires and passions.

We experience big changes in our views on life, our goals, and our ideas of what makes us successful and happy as we become more in tune with who we really are. Things that were once important may lose their shine, and new, more satisfying ways may open up. This adjustment can be hard because it often forces us to leave our comfort zones, face our fears, and deal with the misunderstood or disapproved of people around us. However, it is in this place of alignment that we feel truly fulfilled and like our lives have a purpose.

Accepting and loving who we are, flaws and all is part of being our true selves. It means letting go of the persona we have made up to fit different jobs and accepting our quirks, strengths, and weaknesses as they are. That acceptance is not a sign of laziness; rather, it is an understanding that real growth and happiness come from being ourselves instead of trying to please other people.

Stepping into our true selves is ultimately a freeing and powerful experience. It sets us free from the chains of pretending and lets us live more freely, honestly, and joyfully. When we start down this road, we not only change the purpose and direction of our lives, but we also attract chances, people, and experiences that are in line with who we really are. Being truly ourselves is an ongoing process that leads to a life that is not only lived but fully accepted in all its beauty and authenticity.

Chapter 6

Living my Authentic Life Journey

By the end of May, I had created Authentic Life Journey and began envisioning what I wanted to create through this company. It was easy to see what I wanted to do—coaching, energy work, yoga, meditation, retreats, training, programs and more.

In the beginning, I could see everything so clearly but there was some uncertainty about how to create some aspects of my vision. That rigid mind was showing up once again. The struggle is real no matter where we are on our journey. We have some things that just keep showing up so we can shed more and more layers and heal these samskaras, or shadows of ourselves.

This work is a huge part of my healing journey and one that is actually my greatest opportunity to expand and grow. We sometimes get stuck thinking, "Oh I'm supposed to be all love and light and my problems just go away" but that's just not how it works.

The shadows or dark sides of ourselves are where the work in self-exploration is the greatest gift. This was the phrase that settled into me when I began to feel frustrated with my rigid mind or when my self-deprecating thoughts and actions showed up:

"What is the gift of this experience, feeling, or situation? "

The gift was actually how I began to love my shadows and treat them with gentleness and kindness. My heart whispered into my awareness that my shadows truly needed to be accepted for real healing to come. Wow, what a huge load off to be able to make friends with these aspects of me that I treated so poorly and felt were bad. They are not bad or a reason to abuse me. Rather, they are actually my soul's call to action to bring more love to myself.

As I loved myself more, I began to soften and become more open. Open to more love, opportunities, connections, and experiences—just more! More of anything that my limited mindset couldn't find its way to seeing as possible.

The possibilities became abundant once I opened myself to healing and loving myself. This was the core of the Authentic Life Journey! This was the doorway to finding my way to adventure, spiritual growth, leaps of faith and so much travel! The thing that I dreamed of all the time was exploring and seeing the world.

I believed now it was possible, I could go anywhere I wanted and it was accessible. Little did I know in this early stage of envisioning my business and life what was to come just because I began to honor the gifts of healing.

Insight: Embracing authenticity in our daily lives invites a deeper connection with ourselves and others, fostering a more fulfilling and meaningful existence.

Authenticity in our daily lives takes guts and the ability to accept ourselves. In order to meet the standards set by society, our friends, or even our own standards, we have to take off the masks we usually wear. Real living means staying true to our views, values, and emotions, even if they are different from what other people think or feel. It is about being brave enough to say what we think, stick to our beliefs, and be honest about our flaws and fears. By doing this, we not only improve our relationship with ourselves, but we also make bonds with other people that are deeper and more real.

An even deeper sense of freedom comes from living in an honest way. Having the freedom to be ourselves without worrying about being judged or rejected is a great feeling. This freedom also includes the choices and decisions we make, since our inner compass guides us more than outside forces. When our acts are in line with who we really are, our lives become more in sync and peaceful. Having this consistency makes us happy and at peace because we are not fighting with ourselves to be someone we are not.

Also, being real helps people connect with you more deeply. Being real makes it okay for other people to do the same. People can be truly themselves when they trust and respect each other and feel safe enough to say what they really think and feel. There is no pretense or shallowness in these exchanges, which makes room for deeper and more satisfying relationships. Being honest makes our contacts better and helps us understand each other better, whether we are in a personal relationship, at work, or just out for a coffee.

It is not always easy, though, to be real. It can be hard, especially in a world where following the crowd seems like the easy thing to do. One of the fears that comes with being honest is that someone will judge or reject us. Becoming truly yourself has many more benefits than worries. Being honest lets us live our lives the way we want, follow our true interests, and connect deeply with the people and things around us. It is an important part of living a full and worthwhile life, which makes it richer and more vibrant. When we choose to be authentic, we choose to enjoy all of life's difficulties, joys, and complexities.

Chapter 7

Hawaii 2016

I can honestly say I had a few places that I always wanted to visit. In truth, I think it's way more than a few. When I first thought about traveling, there were some very specific places that topped my list. Hawaii was one of those bucket list places I always wanted to go to but didn't really believe it was possible until I ended up there.

For several years prior to 2016, I had found a friendship with Charlotte. We were friends of friends that eventually connected and formed our own friendship. This relationship was crucial in healing some of the deep-rooted shadows that I held around friendships.

I had struggled for many years with my relationships in general but especially in my female friendships. I always seemed to be too much or not enough, and it seemed like I couldn't find lasting friendships. It caused me so much sorrow that I realized I shut down and withdrew because it just felt safer that way.

As Charlotte and I developed our friendship, I noticed that there was a realness in our relationship that was different. I was so grateful for this authentic friendship and the ability to just relax and have fun! It felt good to feel loved, supported, and seen for what felt like the first time in a friendship.

In the summer of 2016, Charlotte felt called to move to Hawaii. While I was happy for her, I was also a little sad to see her go. I knew in my heart this was so good for her. As she began to make her moving plans, she found out her sweet dog, Lucy, would have to wait a period of 2 months, a requirement by the state of Hawaii, to come live with them. Charlotte was not sure how she was going to get Lucy there once the quarantine period was over. Without hesitation, I remember saying that I would fly over with Lucy!

Within a few days, we had booked the flights and it was done. I was going to Hawaii!

I can honestly say if I hadn't already done all the work I had been doing all year it might not have happened. I would have never just jumped right in and volunteered for something like that! I know now that it was exactly the step I was supposed to take.

Takeaway: Serendipitous connections and unexpected opportunities can lead to significant personal growth and lifelong memories.

The secret gems in our lives are often the chance meetings and chances we did not expect. Even though we did not plan or expect these times to happen, they can lead to new experiences, relationships, and insights that have a big effect on our personal growth. As they grow, they tell us that life is unpredictable and that magic can happen when we let it. These connections could be a chance meeting with a stranger that turns into a lifelong friend, a hasty choice that leads to an unforgettable trip, or a chance event that opens up a key job opening. If any of these lucky events happen to us, they could add rich layers to our life story, helping us grow and weaving together a big fabric of our experiences.

It often takes a leap of faith to take advantage of these unexpected chances. Being brave means going with our gut, leaving our comfort zones, and being open to what life has to offer. Although this might be scary, it is often when we are open and unsure that we learn more about ourselves and the world around us. These events make us think about what we think we know, push our limits, and help us grow in ways we might not have expected. They can also help us grow as people as we learn to deal with new situations and adjust to things we did not expect.

Also, these happy accidents often lead to some of the best and most valued memories. These unexpected and new events leave a lasting effect, making our lives better by giving us stories to tell and lessons to learn. They tell us that the journey through life is not just about getting where we want to go; it is also about the stops and detours we do not expect. These things can bring us happiness, laughter, and sometimes deep understanding, giving our lives more color and meaning.

By their very nature, chance meetings and unplanned chances show how beautiful and mysterious life is. Their presence makes us realize how connected all of our journeys are and how the most important experiences do not always come from carefully planned events but from the unexpected. When you go into these times with an open mind and heart, you can grow a lot, learn about yourself, and make experiences that will last a lifetime. These things help us remember to be in the present, enjoy the journey, and be open to all the wonderful things that life has to give.

Chapter 8

Breaking the Foundation

The journey to Hawaii was a long trip from sunny Florida. I had a lot of time to anticipate what was to come. I had absolutely no idea what actually would've happened. I didn't know much about the deep traditions of Hawaiian history, but I can say I felt the deep roots of the Big Island and the great presence of the sacredness of the land during my time there.

It was such a magical experience! From delivering my friend her sweet pup to all of the adventures we took, I was in awe of how much we accomplished in the ten days I was there! We hiked to the volcano, dove off the shore, and drove nearly the entire island just exploring.

The most impactful experience I had was when we went to the southernmost point of the island and found a place where people jumped from the cliff into the Pacific Ocean. The friends we journeyed with went for it, and I thought: "Well, why not?"

I stood there looking over the edge thinking that it was a pretty long jump and had to really decide if I was going to do this – and then I jumped! As I hit the water's edge I felt a sharp pain at the tailbone and thought oh dang what did I do? Thankfully I was able to climb up the ladder but I was definitely feeling discomfort at my tailbone.

I wasn't so hurt that I needed to go to a doctor, but it was clear I bruised or possibly broke my tailbone. Unfortunately, there is not much that can be done when you injure your tailbone other than let it heal! After the jump, we continued onto the green sand beach, and I just managed my discomfort while we drove.

In the days after this experience, I used my tools, including reiki, cupping, and meditation to help the discomfort but continued on and enjoyed my journey. As I had been actively self-exploring, I began to settle into why this injury happened and what was this powerful island trying to teach me.

Through conversations with Charlotte and opening my heart to my own inner knowing, I began to see the answers. As I had just opened up my heart to living an authentic life experience, I could see that it was time to break my very foundation. From there, I could allow seeds to be planted for the new life I was creating.

As part of my work, I offer reiki and yoga. Both of these modalities work alongside the Chakra System. The chakras are energy centers that are aligned along the spine, brain, and head and are associated with different aspects of our physical, mental, emotional & spiritual body.

The base of the body aligns with the Root Chakra, the energy center that is associated with our sense of grounding, support, safety, and what ground we stand upon. As I mentioned, mine was transforming. When we begin to heal and awaken to deeper levels of consciousness, all of our being will rework and reset to align.

I was changing so quickly. I was on this powerful island that shared with me the idea of destruction and creating a new foundation. When looking upon nature as a messenger, we can see how it plays out in our own lives. I really felt connected to this concept and could understand I was excavating, breaking my foundation of belief, and creating a new one to stand firmly upon.

With this new foundation, I left the island with inspiration, joy, and excitement for creating new and inventive ways to connect to the clients and communities I serve!

Lesson: Sometimes, the most profound growth occurs through unexpected challenges and painful experiences that compel us to reevaluate and rebuild our foundations.

Even though they are hard, life's unexpected problems and painful situations often lead to deep personal growth and change. These events can shake our beliefs, values, and views to their core, forcing us to rethink what we believe to be true and important. We have the chance to rebuild ourselves during times of chaos and uncertainty, and we often come out stronger, smarter, and more adaptable than we were before. Rebuilding our roots is not just about getting better or going back to how things were before; it is also about figuring out who we are and what we stand for again.

On the path to rebuilding, we often have to face our fears, insecurities, and the forces we have been avoiding. To go through this process, we need to be honest, brave, and ready to face hard things about our lives and ourselves. We learn more about our patterns, actions, and the ways we have learned to deal with stress through this process. We learn to tell the difference between things that help us grow and things that get in the way of it. By looking inside ourselves, we can build new roots that are based on self-awareness, authenticity, and a stronger sense of purpose.

Also, tough times often push us to learn new skills, ways of looking at things, and ways to deal with stress. Some of us may find strengths and skills we did not know we had, or we may learn to value parts of our lives that we used to take for granted. The toughness we develop during these times shapes our personality and how we deal with future problems and unknowns. When we understand we can handle and get through life's challenges, we feel strong and resilient.

In the end, the hardest things we go through often help us grow the most. These times put us to the test, test our limits, and sometimes break us. On the other hand, they also give us the chance to grow as people and rebuild ourselves in ways that are more in line with who we really are. It is not always easy to go through these kinds of problems, but the growth that comes from them is priceless and makes life richer and more important. This serves as a lesson that even in the worst times, we can change and start over.

Chapter 9

Learning the Art of the Sacred Pause

I came back from the trip to Hawaii and I was on fire. I have found this to be a regular occurrence since then—more to come about that as we unfold this journey. Once I was home, so many things were happening at a pace that I had never experienced before. The lesson that came from this was painful in a different way but equally important. I learned that slow and steady is the way, the gifts are always there for me even if they come with discomfort.

I had just experienced the breaking of my foundation in Hawaii. Imagine a cement foundation that's been broken into rubble and that no longer fits together smoothly and flatly; this is what my life now feels like. I felt shaky and unable to stand firm as the ground beneath me was in turmoil.

This is the image in my mind of my time after returning from Hawaii. I was still settling and didn't quite have a firm footing. In my previous life, I would say yes to just about anything and everything. What I know to be true now is that this is not the authentic way to choose steps forward.

Over the next several years, I found myself in several scenarios in which I said yes instead of taking what I now call the "sacred pause". Several of the experiences I had in which I jumped at an invitation to create or commit to a rental space turned out to be more shadowwork in disguise. These shadows were sent to wake me up to another layer that needed to be given space and nurturing.

With each experience, the difficulties lessened but I was still being called to pause and listen before stepping forward. When one situation didn't work out, I'd feel defeated and wonder what I was doing wrong. I'd have to self-evaluate and allow myself to slow down and connect to what I did that created the experience. I had to learn that this is all I have control over— my part in any experience I'm showing up for.

The "sacred pause" was the message my heart wanted me to hear and asked me to honor. What does this mean you may be asking?

An example of the "sacred pause" is when something comes to me and instead of answering immediately, I have to step back from my ego's excitement and get quiet with myself. I listen to my heart and see if this thing, whatever it may be, is right for me. Does this align with my divine purpose and will it raise me up or create dis-ease for my life?

In the quiet, I can observe and witness my inner knowing. I can meditate and see if I can visualize myself in the opportunity. I can listen to my body and observe how I'm feeling within the physical body. If when I do any or all of these things, I feel light and easy, then I know I'm in alignment, and saying yes will be on the path for my soul's calling and purpose.

Still, even today, I find myself struggling to pause at times. Those times are not producing the intensity that was once experienced when I had not learned to observe, listen and honor my heart.

Reflection: The power of pausing and reflecting before making decisions can lead to more mindful and aligned choices in life.

One strong way to live a more mindful and intentional life is to take a moment to think and reflect before making a choice. Taking a moment to stop can seem counterintuitive in a world where life seems to be moving faster all the time. But it is when we are quiet that we can connect with our inner knowledge and make choices that are more in line with who we really are and our long-term goals. This process of reflection helps us take a step back, look at the whole picture, and think about the good and bad effects of our actions.

When we take a moment to think about our choices, we can examine our reasons, feelings, and the many other things that affect our decisions. Often, the first things we do are based on short-lived feelings, outside forces, or long-standing habits that may not be in our best interests. We can get past these automatic responses and act from a clear, calm place if we take a moment to think about it. This way of thinking helps us make decisions that we are more aware of and that we do not regret. It also helps us act in ways that are consistent with our ideals and principles.

This reflective pause is also a technique that helps you become more self-aware and mindful. It tells us to live in the present and see how our choices affect others and ourselves. By doing this practice regularly, we learn more about our triggers, patterns, and real desires. Being self-aware is very helpful because it helps us handle life's difficulties with more ease and confidence.

In the end, taking time to pause and think is a great way to live a more thoughtful and satisfying life. It gives us the power to stop acting on impulse and make choices that align with our deepest values and goals. Over time, this practice can change how we live our lives, making them more purposeful and intentional. It tells us that the small pause can lead to big growth and understanding, letting us live lives that are not only reactive but also deliberate and reflective.

Chapter 10

A Return Of A Soul Sister In Divine Timing

The journey of the "sacred pause" after Hawaii was just one of many awakenings born in the Fall of 2016. As I shared before, my friendship with Charlotte was a huge leaping-off point to healing some deep wounds in my female relationships.

This leads me to Jody—my best friend from college. We met in Texas in our dorm and became fast friends. She was a soul sister from early on. We just jelled like that. Even though I didn't know the phrase until much later in my life she was indeed my soul sister. I understand now that friendships that connect in that way have a way of being a huge part of your story and healing.

Our friendship spanned from college through marriages, moves, kids, and many adventures together and apart. At one point, we were both exiting or had exited marriages that were not working. We came up with a plan to move her to live with me and my son in Florida and the plan was executed. Little did we know this would actually activate what looked like the end of our friendship.

After several months of living together, she decided to return to Texas. When this happened I was devastated. I had experienced endings of relationships before, and they never felt good, but this one broke my heart in a way I couldn't explain or understand.

Over the years after, I would dream of her and even try to connect and see if we could repair our friendship. It just never felt real. After a great deal of mourning, I came to the acceptance that maybe we were just not meant to know each other anymore.

Fast forward to the summer of 2016. I had a statue that Jody had given me, and I knew I needed to let it go. My friendship with Charlotte had taught me to trust again and so I felt called to let the statue go and give it forward to Charlotte. The soul sisters statue deserved to be held in a place of love, and I knew gifting it to Charlotte would give me a way to let go with love.

At the same time, I gave the statue to Charlotte, I had been inspired to have a sacred releasing ceremony. I felt called to offer my gratitude to Jody and for our friendship. I then asked the Divine to release me of my sorrow and yearning for us to have our friendship again. I prayed and visualized myself freed from our bond and I let go.

To my great surprise, about 3 weeks later, she reached out to me and wanted to talk. I was in shock and awe. This was unbelievable to my ego mind, but my heart knew better than me! When I really let go, that set in motion this repair that I never thought possible! We spoke that day and then over the next six to eight months we would talk from time to time.

In the summer of 2017, a lot happened that was very challenging for me; hence, the learning of the "sacred pause". Jody and I were finding more and more comfort with each other, talking over text more often and ultimately finding a new friendship built on a new foundation.

That August, I was really feeling the need to see her in person and so we discussed my coming for a visit. Labor Day weekend was the date we settled on, and it was all set. I was ready to journey to Las Vegas once again.

Other than my home in Florida and living in Dallas/Fort Worth for college and a short while after, I've not been anywhere else as much as Las Vegas. I've had several friends move there, two of whom I rode out with when they moved. Las Vegas feels like a second home to me at this point!

So here I go again to Las Vegas to reconnect with my friend. This was a most powerful journey for me because we were building a new friendship on a new foundation after a very long and curvy road. I wasn't sure how it would feel to see her in person now that we were healing, but as soon as we saw each other in the baggage claim it was like nothing ever happened.

My soul sister and I were together again, and my heart was so happy. Now that doesn't mean we didn't have work to do, but our hearts knew everything was ok and would be no matter what.

The journey of letting go is the most difficult and can be the most rewarding all at the same time. This trip was just the beginning, and we once again would adventure and support one another but this time in a more authentic way.

Seeing that we were able to have such a hard ending and, in divine order and time, return to one another is a testimony to how powerful this work that I was doing really is. When I trust my heart and the Divine messages all that's supposed to be will be.

The lesson of letting go and trusting in the Divine order and timing of all things was necessary. Not only for my relationship but for my journey forward. As we now know, my rigid mind can be a great adversary, but learning to trust in the Divine is ultimately the gift here and the one I'm most grateful for.

Insight: Rekindling old friendships can bring healing and closure, reminding us that relationships can evolve and transform over time.

Getting back in touch with old friends is often a unique way to heal and move on. We all go through different things in life, and over time, old friends may grow apart. Getting these links going again, on the other hand, can be a powerful reminder of how relationships last a lifetime and how they can change and grow over time. When you see an old friend again, it can make you feel nostalgic, bring back memories, and make you think about how far you have both come. It is a chance to talk about the good and bad things that have happened in your lives and to see each other in a new way, based on what each person has been through since the last time you met.

Getting back in touch with these old friends often leads to surprising discoveries and new ideas. It can show how much each person has changed and grown over time, showing new parts of their personality and character. It also makes it possible to clear up problems or mistakes from the past. When you go back to old arguments with the knowledge and experience you have gained over the years, you can help people forgive and understand each other better. What could have been a source of sorrow can become a way for you to grow as a person.

Also, getting back in touch with old friends can make our social networks stronger. These ties give us a unique link to our past, keeping us grounded in history while also making our present lives better. They keep our lives going, make us feel like we belong, and connect us to times in our lives that might feel far away otherwise. Getting back in touch with old friends can also bring you comfort and stability because these friendships often have a foundational quality that younger ones may not have yet.

In the end, getting old friends back together is not just about remembering the past; it is also about connecting the past to the present. It means recognizing that even though relationships change over time, the tie that was there before can still be important and valuable. This process can help us heal by giving us closure, new insights, and a greater understanding of the relationships that have shaped our lives. This is a good lesson that friendships, like life, are fluid and always changing. There is always room for improvement, understanding, and getting back in touch.

Chapter 11

Tucson to Sedona
a Practice in Patience

In 2017, I took several adventures, some with my family and others with myself and friends. After my quick trip to Las Vegas, I was heading out to a training in Tucson, AZ, and decided well if I'm going to be in Arizona I need to experience Sedona!

The trip began with a great deal of difficulty because 2 days before I was to fly out to Arizona, a hurricane came through and affected our city enough that the airport closed. Luckily my husband was willing to drive me to Atlanta to catch a flight out on time to get to my training. This was probably a sign of getting comfortable with things not going perfectly smoothly.

Once I arrived in Phoenix, I got my rental car and began the drive to Tucson, lots of driving, but I was excited to explore. I arrived with ease at my hotel and had a wonderful 4-day training.

At the end of the last day, I was eager to get on the road and head back to Phoenix to collect my friend Erin who was flying in to join me and continue on to Sedona. I got into the car, hit up a coffee shop for a beverage, and headed to the highway. I didn't set the GPS because it was a direct route and I had felt comfortable with getting to the highway and the airport without it.

I got on the highway and about 10 minutes down the road, the traffic was at a dead stop. I immediately opened my GPS, and there was a solid red for miles ahead of me. There was no way to exit the highway. I was stuck. I immediately communicated this with my friend Erin as she was landing and expecting me to be there upon her arrival.

Once she landed, we began the discussion of what to do. It was clear to me I wasn't going anywhere fast. After several hours sitting on the highway and communicating with Erin we decided she should get a room near the airport because I had no indication of when I may arrive.

My patience level was being challenged indeed, and my rigid mind was so upset. I took some deep breaths and moved through the discomfort, and then another wave would come. At one point, I was grateful for the beverage I got because it was gone, and I had to use the cup in another way! I was stuck and had to be patient.

Patience has not been one of my greatest virtues, and clearly, my spirit was ready for me to face the lesson directly! After approximately 7 hours, my car made it up to the exit that everyone had been funneling onto all day, and just as I came up to the exit, an officer was pulling the cones and waving me through to the highway that was now open once again!

No one was in front of me for nearly half the trip to Phoenix, and my path was clear and easy for the rest of the drive to the hotel. Once I arrived, I dove into the bed and passed out.

In the morning, we collected ourselves, grabbed food, and finally hit the road to Sedona. We discussed the craziness of the day before, and I felt grateful for Erin's willingness to go with the flow and offer her patience to me as I was learning my lesson in patience.

We pulled off at the exit to head to Sedona and were excited and filled with anticipation. At one point, we felt the energy shift as we entered the outskirts of the town. We suddenly saw in front of us the grand Red Rocks and couldn't believe our eyes.

Upon reflection, we discussed the fact that had we made it the night before, we would have missed the view because it would have been night already!

This is when the lesson in patience really kicked in, if there had been nothing holding me up until 11 pm, we would have missed this! Immediately, gratitude entered my being and I took in the awareness of the importance of patience when things aren't going according to my timetable. I still have to work the edges of patience, but I do recall this story when I'm feeling extra attached to my timing.

Takeaway: Patience is not just a virtue but a necessary practice that allows us to appreciate the journey and find meaning in unexpected detours.

People often praise patience as a virtue, but what really makes it valuable is that it is a key skill for living a full life. In a world that often values speed and getting things right away, patience tells us to take our time and enjoy the little things along the way. It lets us fully feel and understand what we are doing instead of rushing through it to get to the next thing. Being patient does not mean just waiting; it means being in the present moment, realizing that some things can not be rushed, and realizing that forward movement often takes time.

Being patient is especially important when life takes us in unexpected directions. It can be stressful and discouraging to have to deal with problems, delays, or changes in direction. However, if you are patient, they can also lead to new ideas and growth opportunities you did not expect. Patience helps us handle these delays with ease and openness, and it helps us find lessons and meaning in these changes from our original plan. As a result, we learn to be flexible, to change our goals, and to enjoy and value the trip itself, not just the end goal.

Besides that, being patient makes you feel more thankful and satisfied. We are more likely to enjoy the little wins and easy pleasures of life when we are patient. We become better listeners, more understanding friends, and more careful decision-makers. Patience also helps us feel less stressed and anxious because it teaches us to accept things we can not change and focus on the things we can. We can have a more peaceful and grateful view of life if we learn to be patient.

Basically, being patient is a skill that makes our lives better. It is a recognition that life's best moments usually happen when things happen at their own pace. We learn to enjoy the road and handle its ups and downs with grace and strength when we are patient. We can find meaning in the unexpected, grow through difficulties, and enjoy the unique pace of our own life's journey when we do this. Being patient helps us remember that every moment is a chance to grow as a person, and every step, no matter how small or slow, is important.

Chapter 12

The Gifts of Co-Creating

As I returned from Arizona I had clarity of my direction and was ready to root in some of the ideas and inspiration that I had been dreaming of. I had some amazing co-creators showing up that would support the visions to come together. This concept of co-creating was a central message that I had been hearing from the first sparks of inspiration for Authentic Life Journey. I knew this was going to be an important aspect of my vision for this company in so many ways.

In the coming years, I co-created in so many ways with some truly magical creators. As with all of my experiences, I saw many shadows showing up that would need to be given attention and I was finding more ease with those relationships for I had awareness. Awareness is one of the first key tools I share in my coaching work because without the eye of the observer how can we develop an understanding of where we may need to shine the light of love?

This time in my journey became the time I was truly learning to live with awareness and how to honor what I was gaining insight into. Some of the insight was very uplifting and felt like sunlight. While other experiences were stirring up so much chaos and dis-ease I could barely see how to find my way out of the darkness. No matter the outcome of the many collaborations I was learning and growing and becoming a better version of myself each step.

As the opportunities continued to arise I gained some of the greatest insights I could have asked for. Each shadow that showed up was an opportunity to heal and eventually, I could find gratitude for the teachers that came to my side to push me forward. It's so easy to find gratitude for the light and easeful people in our lives but to learn to hold gratitude for those that challenged you or that brought about experiences that one could call hurtful is where the real magic of healing was found for me.

Diving deeper and deeper into my healing I found myself moving closer to my authentic heart and voice. Those relationships would span from a simple collaborator all the way to my closest family members, the greatest teachers of all. The tool of gratitude ultimately gave me the key to healing one of my greatest life lessons, feeling abandonment. This was a struggle I can say I have experienced for the better part of my adult life.

Abandonment became my gift and gratitude its key. In my early thirties, I worked with a counselor after so much loss had occurred, and I couldn't find any ease. She offered me a word that shined a light on why I was so lost, Codependency. This introduction to codependency took me down a path of reading and finding support that I knew was a light in the darkness. Codependency was the root of my abandonment feelings and would take me gently towards healing over many years.

It wasn't until my early forties that I really found ease around my abandonment issues and therefore my codependency. I was in awareness over the time between the counselors first opening my eyes and heart to this issue and the day gratitude gave me the deepest healing I can remember in regards to my abandonment issues. Each of the relationships I had that offered challenges or shadows to arise was a part of this ongoing healing.

Until one can find a mindset shift to gaze upon your life as an opportunity, it's almost impossible to find the light. For me, this shift was the way to see it all as a gift. In February 2020 I was co-leading a workshop on Gratitude and it was at this workshop that gratitude once again ignited some of the most powerful healing to this day.

As part of the workshop, we asked the participants to write down all the pain they were feeling in their lives. Whatever was a common theme or a constant issue that showed up over and over. I too felt called to jot down the experiences I'd like to honor and open my heart to. The subject of feeling abandoned was one of the items on my list. The next step we guided them was to write a letter of gratitude to the people and experiences that were a part of these issues offering gratitude for the gift the person or experience gave them.

When I began to write my letter it just flew out of my hand, for every person that I felt abandoned by I turned the sadness into gratitude. As I wrote each thing that was done that caused me to feel abandoned I wrote "Thank You For The Gift Of...." and I listed out everything. Once I wrote these pains as gifts I could clearly see that the sadness was not serving me because the gifts were actions that were not in alignment with what I was learning real authentic friendship looked and felt like. It freed me from the binds of feeling abandoned and ultimately gave me a reason to focus on the people in my life who were showing up! In truth, the energy I spent on feeling sad about the losses was taking away the joy of what I actually had.

This healing taught me the concept of alignment and learning to honor the flow of relationships and honor the concept of friendships coming to you for a reason, a season, and a lifetime. In direct opposition to the co-creators and relationships that were born of my codependency, I also gained insight from the co-creators and collaborators that showed me what authentic friendship and collaboration were.

This is where my journey in the darkness became the fuel to the life and relationships that I found through healing. Does that mean I don't have more lessons with these friendships, of course not, but I know that I can show up as a goddess one day and complete a mess the next and they will just hold space for me. The journey of creating with friends I'm in heart alignment with is one of great joy. As I healed and began to envision the relationships I wanted in my life they showed up in spades!

The collaborations that have come my way since I have been more aware and learned how to pause, lean in, and feel the heart of another have been some of the most magical experiences. Between Yoga Teacher Training, Divine Heart Magic Women's Circle, Invoking the Divine Goddess, leading workshops and retreats, and so much more, I found my heart song and I have been singing her lyrics ever since.

Lesson: Collaboration and co-creation can open new avenues for personal growth and lead to fulfilling partnerships and projects.

Working together and making things together are great ways to grow as a person and in your career. We are more open to new ideas, views, and ways of thinking when we work with other people. When we work together and share our knowledge, skills, and ideas, we can come up with new ideas and undertake creative projects that would be hard to complete on our own. People who work together are more likely to share their knowledge and combine their different skills, which creates unity where the whole is greater than the sum of its parts.

Co-creation also teaches us important lessons about how to communicate, find common ground, and value different points of view. It forces us to be clear about what we think, pay attention to what others have to say, and be open to helpful criticism. Working together teaches us how to negotiate and how important it is to find shared ground. These skills are very useful in both personal and business situations because they help people get along and respect each other. When we work closely with others, we learn about their experiences and backgrounds, which makes us more empathetic. This can help us see things from a wider perspective and improve our emotional intelligence.

Working together also often helps us find hidden talents we did not know we had. It gets us out of our comfort zones and makes us want to try new things and take risks. Because we are working together, we might discover secret skills or find new interests. The sense of accomplishment and satisfaction that comes from working together to complete a job is very satisfying. The process of working together, facing problems, and learning from each other is what makes the experience more valuable, not just the end result.

Collaboration and co-creation are not just about sharing resources; they are also about making friends and feeling like you are part of a group. When people work together on projects, whether they are for work, the community, or the arts, they can form valuable partnerships and achieve important results. These things tell us that we are stronger and more capable when we work together and use all of our skills to make something truly amazing. Accepting the idea of working together not only helps us grow as people, but it also makes the world more creative and linked.

Chapter 13

Creative Expression at Indian Shores Beach Journeys

The first of the co-creations that I opened up to once I had returned from Arizona was when I committed to leading a Yoga Teacher Training. This had been something in the works prior to the trip but it hadn't really taken form because spirit was helping work through some deep shadows earlier that year. I was frustrated when it wasn't coming together and then when it did I could see why. When Erin and I traveled to Sedona and the Grand Canyon we had a lot of time to talk and be in union with each other. I knew then it was time to get it together and get this training realized.

We had already committed to a date, but I was still dragging on the process we needed to get things together. The previous year I had put together the base of the training while staying at my friend's condo. This was a place where I found great inspiration and wrote a lot over the years and I knew it was necessary to return as more creativity was boiling. Over the next several months I traveled to the beach once a month to write and create this program. My co-creators worked on their parts and a little at a time it began to form.

As I traveled to the condo, I found so much freedom and expansion happening. For the first time, I began to own my strengths and open my heart to the idea that I am a creative person and that creativity is a gift from the divine. I knew I had some creativity with me as in my previous life experience, I was a Theater Major, but this was different. I began to understand that as a channel for the divine to speak through me, I was able to co-create with spirit.

This concept of co-creating with the divine was shared with me through a beautiful collaborator and friend Su. This time I spent at the beach ended up being a much grander experience than I saw it to be at first. It was over this time that Su re-entered my life and what came next was nothing less than divine heart magic!

Reflection: Creative expression is a powerful tool for self-discovery and can often lead to profound personal insights and breakthroughs.

Expressing ourselves creatively is a way to get to know ourselves better. We can look at our ideas, feelings, and experiences through a new lens, which often leads to deep personal insights. Whether we show ourselves through writing, painting, music, dance, or some other form of art, we can say things that might be hard to say with words alone. It helps us express our deepest feelings and thoughts to others, giving shape to the vague and making the intangible parts of our experiences real.

As we do artistic things, we often learn more about ourselves and how we fit into the world. When we write, we might find out about secret parts of our personalities, unresolved feelings, or new ways of looking at things that happened in the past. This process can be helpful because it can help you let go of stress and work through complicated feelings. Expressing ourselves creatively also helps us connect with our intuition and imagination, which can lead to new ways of thinking and fixing problems. It forces us to think outside the box and discover new ideas by pushing the limits of how we normally think.

Also, being creative is not just about what you make; it is also about the way you make it. Making art can be a mindful and meditative practice that helps us connect with our real selves and live in the present moment. When we are in a state of "flow," where we lose ourselves in an activity, it can be very relaxing and satisfying. At this point, time seems to have stopped, and we are fully focused on our artistic work. This kind of immersion can make you feel happy and fulfilled, and it can even help you have deep emotional breakthroughs and insights.

To sum up, being creative is a strong way to learn about yourself and grow. It lets us explore the depths of our minds in a healthy and safe way, giving us a way to let out our feelings and express ourselves. When we connect with our creative selves, we can learn more about who we are and where we fit in the world. Creative expression is a trip worth taking, whether it is a hobby or a job. It opens up a world of possibilities for discovery, healing, and change.

Chapter 14

Asking For Help

In addition to this time being a very expansive and creative time it also continued to be a time of deep soul search and healing. I found myself working through layer upon layer of self-healing and explorations. There were moments I cried out for it to slow down, and other times I was at peace with the intensity of the process. It seemed that I was on a fast track over the 3 years or so since I found my way to Authentic Life Journey and the pedal was all the way to the floor. It was as if the spirit was saying "Ok you're awake let's do this!"

At some point in early December of 2018, I remember being so very challenged and I wanted to get off the train but I knew I couldn't turn away from my purpose. I was awakened and I was walking through a fire, a fire I needed to walk through to find my heart open and ready to step out in a way that spirit had built me for. I was so uncomfortable and I needed help. One Friday morning I was sitting in my car outside my office before entering to lead a yoga class and I was crying out and praying for help. I didn't know how the help would show up but I asked and would be open to how help would show up.

Within 1 hour my phone had a text message on it from my dear friend Su. I hadn't seen her in nearly 9 months or so and then suddenly she was there. This was very common for us, we both had busy lives but when we were to be together it was always divine and easeful. She was messaging me about the intentions she had received earlier in the month, from our intention-setting session. Every year I lead an intention-setting session in January and in December I send out the letters the participants wrote to themselves at the workshop. I was sure this was my answer from the divine.

I messaged her back after my class and asked if we could talk and if she might be available to offer me a reiki session. We found a way on a call and discussed my current dis-ease and I shared with her my prayers and her contacting me within an hour of the request for help. We both knew this was divine timing and she made space for me two days later. She came and shared the reiki session with me and the shift that came after was exactly what I needed.

A few weeks later we scheduled time to meet and discuss the potential of co-creating more events and this was the beginning of what became the Divine Heart Magic Women's Circle and our renewed connection to co-creating.

Insight: Recognizing the need for help and being open to receiving it is a sign of strength, not weakness, and can lead to transformative support and healing.

A big part of growing and healing is realizing that you need help and being willing to accept it. Often, social norms and pride can make it hard to ask for help, because many people see it as a sign of weakness. Recognizing your weaknesses or problems and asking for help, on the other hand, is a sign of great strength and self-awareness. It shows that you want to improve, know that we all count on each other, and understand that no one should have to handle the challenges of life by themselves.

There are different ways to be willing to accept help. It could mean getting mental support from family or friends, going to therapy or counseling, or even asking for help with things around the house when you need it. Because we are open, we can learn from the knowledge, experience, and kindness of others, which gives us new ideas and ways to deal with our problems. It also makes room for being open and real connection, which leads to stronger bonds based on trust and helping each other.

Also, asking for help can be a life-changing event. It can help us grow as people by teaching us new ways to deal with problems, giving us new insights into how we act, and making us stronger. This process of healing and getting help is not just about fixing a problem; it is about growing as people. It teaches us how to be kind to ourselves, how important society is, and how powerful empathy can be. By accepting the help that is out there, we are better able to get through tough times and come out stronger and ready to take on new tasks.

In the end, realizing that you need help and being willing to accept it shows how brave and dedicated you are to your own health. It is a recognition that growth often needs help from outside sources and that working together and sharing knowledge is powerful. This idea is very important for creating a network of support and a place where asking for help is not seen as a sign of weakness but as an important part of being human. It reminds us that we are stronger when we work together and fosters an atmosphere of care, understanding, and growth for everyone.

Chapter 15

Finding Divine Heart Magic

Su and I had found a rhythm with our co-creations through a combination of a meet-up group and my existing client base. We actively pursued the opportunity to co-create with one another. In February each year, I travel with my husband on a cruise for his work. Many times while I'm on the ship I have great inspirations and I'm returning home with excitement for the inspiration to be created. In 2019 I had an inspiration for a woman's circle to be created. I was already feeling the stirrings to connect to my divine feminine self more to work on healing my imbalances. The call to action for a woman's circle was in direct alignment with that path.

As soon as I returned I reached out to Su and asked her thoughts on my idea and she was ecstatic to join me. The name of our circle became the Divine Heart Magic Woman's Circle. This became an amazing outlet for us and offered an amazing opportunity to meet other women seeking the same things we were, to remember our divine feminine self and the magic we are here to share.

Su and I were inspired every time we came together with this circle and we began to feel the stirrings to create even more of our divine heart magic.

As I sat with this vision and really began to lean into what divine heart magic means to me I was finding access to parts of myself I had hidden and the abundance of creative vision sprung open. I truly believe this group and the experiences we were having together were exactly what I needed to heal and step even further forward on my path.

Once the pandemic happened in 2020 there was a change in the focus of divine heart magic and Su and I found there was much more to be done with this vision. We began to meet regularly to co-create and hold space for what is to be manifested through the lens of Divine Heart Magic. We hold the vision of what will come and continue to experience our own healing all while creating the new. For it is through the healing that the new ideas and inspiration will form.

Takeaway: Connecting with our divine essence and embracing the magic within us can lead to a deeper understanding of our true nature and purpose.

To connect with our divine spirit, we have to go deep inside ourselves. There, we can find the core of our true nature and purpose. This link is not just about knowing yourself; it is a deep understanding that you are a part of something bigger and more complex than your own life. It is realizing that each of us has a unique spark of the divine, a source of love, knowledge, and creativity that goes beyond our physical lives. As we accept our inner magic, we discover new options and see ourselves and the world around us with more wonder and understanding.

Connecting with our divine essence usually includes deep self-reflection and spiritual practices like mindfulness, meditation, and reflective contemplation. These activities help us tune out the noise of our busy lives and make room for the soft words of our inner selves. We can find our inner wants, fears, and truths in this space, which helps us become more in tune with who we really are. This alignment gives us a sense of unity and purpose, which helps us decide what to do and how to do it.

Not only that, but accepting our inner magic and divinity can completely change how we see our lives and our places in the world. It tells us to live with purpose, follow paths that are in line with our deepest values, and interact with the world in a way that shows how we see ourselves as linked to everything else. When we look at things this way, we feel responsible to not only grow ourselves but also make the world a better place.

In conclusion, getting in touch with our divine spirit is a powerful and enlightening experience. It tells us to look deeper into things and find the inner truths of our lives. It helps us remember that we are not just watching our lives happen; we are also taking part in a bigger dance happening in the universe. When we accept the magic that exists within us, we create a life that has more meaning, joy, and satisfaction, based on a deep understanding of who we are and what we are here to do. This connection is an ongoing journey that makes life more interesting and helps us learn more about the world and our place in it.

Chapter 16

Goddesses Unite

In 2016 when I launched Authentic Life Journey I launched alongside it the ALJ Mindfulness Coaching Program. This was a part of the vision I had from the beginning and in truth was the catalyst to rebranding my company and vision to Authentic Life Journey. Once I created the content for the program I began to offer group sessions to help me work through the program with others and re-work anything that needed to be shifted.

I was working with a studio about an hour from me offering sound healings and workshops and I suggested we offer the program to their community. We began to market the program and one day I received a call from a woman that found the program and wanted to speak with me. I called her back and communicated with her. Dawn was a bubbly and highly energetic person. She had a friend, Paige, whom she knew needed to participate in my program and she wanted more information. I said to her "Well that's so lovely you are looking out for your friend but if she wants to participate she will need to call me" within a day Paige called.

Paige signed up just shortly after we spoke and then the class was never booked by anyone else. I called her and asked how she felt about working together privately. She was open to it so we scheduled her first session. Paige is an amazing person and has a magical story of her own to tell but in my story, she became my first coaching client. She was an excellent person for me to work through some of my kinks with, as she is a go-with-the-flow kind of person.

We worked together through the foundation program and beyond. My first private client was a successful journey. Little did I know that the divine brought us together for more than just this one moment. After working together for two years Paige moved and our dynamic changed. We would meet online and this opened up another aspect of my work which I had no idea how I'd get here.

In late 2018 she decided to join my second Yoga Teacher Training class and we shifted from private sessions to her participation in the program. At the end of the training, I had this nudge to ask her if she wanted to discuss working together on a project I was feeling called to open my heart to. She agreed to discuss it, and we scheduled a time to meet. In September 2019, we met at her house in Jacksonville Beach and began to envision Invoking The Divine Goddess. This work would support me in ways that I couldn't begin to explain, this is where I really began to find my divine feminine love.

We have had many experiences with the vision from online groups and a weekly YouTube talk to destination retreats. We now are focusing our energy on retreats to bring goddesses together to commune with nature, other goddesses, and ultimately, themselves.

Takeaway: Connecting with our divine essence and embracing the magic within us can lead to a deeper understanding of our true nature and purpose.

Adoring the divine feminine inside means recognizing and integrating the traits usually connected with female energy, like intuition, kindness, nurturing, and creativity. This journey is important for people of all genders because it balances out the masculine traits that are often dominating, such as logic, competition, and assertiveness. By accepting these parts of themselves, people can have a fuller experience of who they are, which makes them feel complete. The process is very personal, but it works best when there are other people who understand and support you and share your stories.

It can be very powerful to start or join groups that honor the divine feminine. There is no fear of judgment in these communities, so people can discover and express who they are. They offer rituals, talks, and activities that celebrate the divine feminine that members can do together. This makes it easier for members to connect with these energies. People in these groups share their stories and experiences, pass on their knowledge, and work to make the group stronger as a whole. These groups can give people a strong sense of connection and understanding, which can boost their confidence in their spiritual and personal journey.

Also, these groups help people grow spiritually and personally. They urge their members to go deeper into their spiritual practices, look at things from different points of view, and start journeys of self-discovery. People who are part of these groups often feel supported and encouraged to take big steps in their personal lives, like following their interests, fighting for change, or making their relationships healthier. When a group works together to nurture the divine feminine, it can bring about big changes in both the people and the community as a whole.

In the end, accepting the divine feminine and finding family in groups that support you are two important parts of becoming personally and spiritually whole. In addition to offering support, these groups set off a chain reaction of strength, healing, and change. They tell us that we can make big changes in ourselves and the world around us if we all stand together to honor our deepest truths and help each other on our paths. This method of working together and caring for each other shows how strong and beautiful the divine feminine is, and how important it is for making the world balanced and peaceful.

Chapter 17

Soul Sisters

Paige and I had worked together as coach and client for some time before we had an ah-ha moment. She came to me and shared that she and her friend Dawn were working together with some other women to create. She was sharing with me some of the experiences she had when she mentioned one of the collaborators' names was Su! I said, "Wait, what?" I drilled in a little further and sure enough, her Su was my friend Su.

It's quite magical when you sit back and trust the divine to bring together just what you need. In truth, this is the best practice to trust in the process. We of course sent our friend a picture of us together and well as they say the rest is history! This was a leaping point to what is now a tremendously supportive circle of goddess sisters.

Over the next years, we would commune together and independently with each other which ultimately led to the first Invoking the Divine Goddess Retreat.

As Paige and I began to envision the retreat we decided to hold it in Jacksonville Beach close to where he was living. In fact, it ended up being the house directly across the street from the home they had just purchased. We started the process of sending out the details for the retreat and our group came together. Paige and I were elated that we had this beautiful group coming together.

This retreat was held in January of 2020 and this group of goddesses found such a bond that it carried on well beyond this one weekend together. Our friend Su was the first to register and her presence with us solidified the bond we all had. In addition, we had some new friends join us. We spent a very magical weekend together to open our hearts and surface what we need to create our intentions for the coming year. Little did we know at that time that this community of women would become a sacred soul sister circle.

As the world shut down we leaned into one another and found support and healing as we would meet on Zoom regularly to check in and confirm everyone was doing well, physically, mentally, and emotionally. This was such a gift to my life as I had been working for the prior four years on trusting my friendships and inviting vulnerability to the forefront of my life. This key practice was the balm to soothe me and heal me. The coming together of these women has been one of my greatest gifts.

We came together for a second retreat in 2021 and then I was given the opportunity to share one more round of Yoga Teacher Training with three of these magical goddesses. The uniting of these souls has offered us all friendship, love, and support that we didn't even know we needed until it showed up.

We are all still connected in one way or another and when we need help we know just where to reach out to find a helping hand.

Reflection: Deep and authentic connections with others can provide invaluable support and perspective, enriching our lives in countless ways.

Our emotional and mental health depend on having deep, real relationships with other people. These relationships are deeper than just talking to each other; they involve real understanding, empathy, and respect for each other. To build connections based on authenticity, we need to make sure that both people feel safe enough to be themselves around us. These relationships are like a mirror that helps us see ourselves more clearly and understand our own feelings, thoughts, and actions better. They give us a place to talk about our thoughts and feelings, which can help us see things in new ways that we might not have thought of before.

Real relationships also give people a sense of community and belonging, which is an important part of being human. In a world where being alone and lonely is becoming more common, having a network of supporting relationships can make a big difference in how happy and satisfied we are with our lives. These connections can help you feel better when things are hard by giving you the emotional support and encouragement you need to get through life's obstacles. They help us remember that we are not going through this trip alone, which supports the idea that having similar experiences and helping each other out are important parts of being human.

Additionally, real relationships help individuals learn and grow. Instead of judging or criticizing us, they push us to be better people by showing love, understanding, and gentle support. These connections make us want to learn more about the world and ourselves. We want to get out of our comfort zones, try new things, and take on new tasks. This growth does not happen by itself; the strength of our relationships feeds and supports it.

In the end, real, deep relationships with other people make our lives better in a lot of ways. They bring comfort, happiness, understanding, and a feeling of being a part of something. They push us, help us, and make us better. These relationships are important to our health and happiness, not just nice to have. People often value freedom and self-reliance, but it is important to remember the beauty and power of how we all depend on each other. We make the world a better place by caring for and nurturing these deep ties. It makes our own lives better and makes the world a better place for everyone.

Chapter 18

Time in Nature with my Family to Renew the Soul

The summer of 2020 my family and I decided we needed a change of scenery as we were hitting the edge of being stuck at home. I had made the decision to close the doors of my business. With the Pandemic in full swing and things looking as though they were long from over I decided I needed to simplify. I shifted to working from home and utilizing Erin's office space for in-person clients. We were all feeling the heaviness of the pandemic and really needed a reset.

Nature has always been the place my family and I go to for adventure, relaxation, and resetting. Our house was an anxiety-ridden place and we all needed a minute to pause the noise and open up to some peace. So we drove to the mountains of North Carolina for a pause.

My husband is an avid fisherman and he seeks out any opportunity to cast his line and fish. He is an amazing planner and seeks out all the possibilities for our adventure well before we arrive. So he found hiking trails to waterfalls, rivers to fish, and all the magical outings we could want for our trip. My son was grateful to play and explore and found time to feel free to roam.

This trip was a necessary pause and just what we needed. On the last day of our trip, we found out a hurricane was going to be moving through where we lived which would affect our drive. We made a decision to extend our stay and find one more hike. The hike we took on our last day was suggested to us by our friends who offered us to use their family cabin and visit with them as they lived in the same town.

The hike was a bit away from our cabin so we got going early in the morning. My husband found us another waterfall and up to the hiking trail we went. The hike was a bit steeper than the other but in the end was totally worth the extra effort to reach the view at Pickens Nose. You stand on this rock and look out to see thousands of trees. My son and husband were looking from the rock and I was a little further back on the trail. I took this picture which is one of my favorites and still hangs on our wall.

The stillness of the forest and the sturdiness I feel when I look at the picture is inspiring. Stillness is the message the trip offered me, to pause and be still. For in the stillness, I can hear my heart, the divine center and truth of my life. The truth was we were ok. There was so much fear we experienced during that time. Both my husband and I work for ourselves so the two years of the active pandemic took a toll on our sense of safety. This trip and that memory are the answers that get missed so easily in the noise of life, be still, the answers are here.

After this trip, I spent more time in stillness in nature and remembering I'm not alone and all will be ok.

I would spend the next year creating, envisioning, and trusting in the process of it all. This trip was our lesson in pause, trust, and stillness.

Insight: Nature has a unique way of grounding us, offering peace and clarity, and reminding us of the beauty and simplicity of life.

In all of its many forms, nature has an amazing power to settle us and give us a sense of peace that is hard to find in our everyday lives. Away from the constant stream of stimuli that makes up daily life, the natural world is a great place to be. We can calm down, slow down, and get back in touch with the rhythms of the natural world when we are in nature. This link brings me a deep sense of peace and reminds me of how beautiful and simple the world is. Nature can bring us back to the present moment with the soft rustling of leaves in the wind, the rhythmic crashing of ocean waves, or the peaceful quiet of a mountain landscape. It is a safe place to get away from the stress and problems of city life.

Being in nature also helps you see things more clearly. When we get away from the noise and distractions of everyday life, we can see our problems and issues in a new light. Natural places help us think more clearly and artistically because they are simple and clean. Because of their natural beauty and the way they grow, die, and come back to life, nature's processes can help us understand our own lives. It makes us think about how short life's problems are and how time keeps moving forward, which helps us see what really matters.

Plus, being outside is good for more than just our mental and emotional health; it is also good for our bodies. Scientists have found that spending time in nature can lower stress, raise happiness, lower blood pressure, and even boost the immune system. All of these health benefits serve as reminders of how deeply connected we are to nature and how important it is for our health to stay connected.

Nature is a strong partner in our search for peace, clarity, and ease. It gives us a sense of stability, a break from our busy lives, and a connection to the basic facts of life. Natural places are soothing and beautiful, and they help us see how small our lives really are by telling us of the joy and wonder in the world. Getting outside, whether it is for a walk in the park, a hike in the mountains, or just some time in the yard, is a simple but profound way to heal our souls and feel better.

Chapter 19

Manifesting Dreams:
The Family Heads to Hawaii

From the time I went to Hawaii in 2016 my son would talk to me all the time about how he wanted to go to Hawaii after his graduation. I of course was like, sure if we can figure it out I will do what I can. My son's senior year was 2020-2021 so this definitely threw a wrench into the idea. I told him as he started his senior year I knew what he wanted for graduation but I'm not sure if we will be able to make it happen since the world is still on its end. He of course understood and we went about the year with no expectations.

In June things were beginning to open up more and we could see possibilities for travel and such become more accessible. I have throughout the years had dreams where friends of mine would show up. I recalled a dream in January of 2020 where I saw myself, my son, my husband, and Charlotte together in what appeared to be Hawaii standing next to an infinity pool. I remember waking up and texting her immediately. It's such a vivid memory that I have never forgotten the dream. In June 2021 I had another dream of Charlotte, I don't recall this dream as well but I do recall what happened when I woke.

I again messaged her to see how she was doing, only to find out she was about to fly out to return to the mainland that day! We communicated about a few things and then went on with our day. Not long after that I felt nudged to ask her if she might be open for a visit later in the summer once she returned and her response was "Sure, When?' We began to discuss some dates and landed on them and I began the search for flights and such. I was feeling so inspired at that moment to get it done and so I did. I booked flights within 24 hours and we were set to make my son's dream true. The important thing to note here is that this all happened on June 14th, a date I'll never forget now. I'll share more about that later.

Takeaway: Pursuing dreams and creating memorable experiences with loved ones enriches our lives and strengthens our bonds.

Following your dreams and making memories with people you care about are important parts of living a full life. These shared moments and accomplishments are not just about the events themselves; they also help people connect with each other in deeper ways. People close to us can share joy, learn, and grow with us when we work together to make our dreams come true or even when we bring them along on our own personal quests. These events can be small, everyday things or big, exciting adventures, but they all have a big effect on us and leave deep marks in our hearts and minds.

Our relationships have a special sense of fun and excitement when we share experiences together, especially ones that involve following our dreams or going to new places. To break up the boredom, they push us to leave our comfort zones and see the world in new and exciting ways. Whether we are going to new places, working together on a project, or just trying out a new activity, these kinds of experiences make our lives more interesting and full. They also help us see different sides of each other, which makes us understand and value our loved ones more.

Also, these trips we all take together often have problems and challenges that, when we face them together, make our bonds stronger. We trust and depend on each other more when we work through problems together, help each other through uncertain times, and celebrate our successes. We learn how important it is to work together, be patient, and keep going even when things get hard. Plus, they tell us that reaching a goal is more fun when we share it with people we care about.

In the end, going after our dreams and making memories with people we care about are not just about the accomplishments or the fun; they are about making our lives and relationships better. These times spent together turn into stories we love, lessons we learn, and the building blocks of stronger, more durable ties. When we share the best things and most satisfying moments in life, they tell us that our loved ones are very important in giving our journey meaning and joy.

Chapter 20

Lesson of Letting Go: The Big Island & Big Changes Coming

As we were moving closer to our trip I realized some interesting things that I hadn't connected to until just before we were heading to Hawaii. The dates I had chosen for our trip were the same dates I had traveled here five years prior and I was getting so many messages in my meditations that a big change was coming while in Hawaii. Once again the island was working her magic already.

Traveling at this time was still kind of complicated but we found our way and arrived safe and well. Our first day there we were tired but did explore a bit before heading to bed. Because of the time change, I was awake at 3 AM and my husband had told me a meteor shower was happening that night. Before we went to bed we attempted to see the meteor shower but it was tremendously cloudy and saw only clouds. So since I was awake at 3 AM I decided to check out the sky once again and sure enough it was clear.

I grabbed a cushion and laid down on the deck, I heard my husband stirring and told him to come out to join me. He did and we laid on the deck and enjoyed the sight of the meteor shower. The longer we were there the more clearly we could see! It was such a magical moment we had on our first night there. As I shared I was nudged to be ready for a big change and I was on the lookout for it. When you watch a pot of water boil it takes a long time to get there and, well, this also applies to magical happenings. The more I looked for the big message the further away it seemed to be.

This trip was very different from my first time here, I had day after day of magical things happening my first time. This time it just seemed to never really come. Now, that being said, I saw some magical things happen for my son and my husband, but my magical things seem to be just out of reach. So I resolved myself to let it go and accept that maybe this time wasn't about me. That was the key: to let it go!

We had such an amazing adventure together, exploring the ocean, and volcanoes, seeing sea turtles, snorkeling, swimming with dolphins – oh, and the Manta Rays!

My one dream experience going back to Hawaii was to go on the Dolphin Swim and Manta Ray tour. These were two different experiences we had. The dolphin swim was so exciting for me because dolphins are one of my spirit animals and I couldn't wait to be in the open water and have them swim near us. Unfortunately, I had a terrible headache that morning and my experience was not as I had dreamt it to be because I was in pain. My son on the other hand was having the time of his life. This brought me great joy and was my resolve for the experience that was to see his joy.

On the last night of our trip, we scheduled the Manta Ray Snorkel. I was so excited for this, and it was just the right amount of excitement to keep my mind in the moment and not feeling sad to be heading home the next day. As we headed out to the location where the Manta Rays came, we spoke to the excursion assistant, who shared with us he had family that lived in our same town in Florida, I can't make this stuff up. He told us the Manta Rays didn't come the previous night and to think good thoughts for our night.

I, of course, closed my eyes and began to envision the Manta Rays coming to see us, and sure enough, as soon as we anchored in, the attendant said there was a ray under the boat. I eagerly got prepared and entered the water. The snorkel with the Manta Ray is experienced by holding on to a platform with the light that attracts the plankton, and then the rays swim up to eat. Since I was one of the first few people in the water, I was positioned at the far end of the platform in the middle.

This placement couldn't have been a better spot. Within a few quick minutes, a Manta Ray swam below us and began to swim up to the light. The way the rays swim up and then back down is in a big circle. They swim up toward the light, and then they become flat with the platform with their belly facing the platform. Then they circle back down to the bottom of the ocean and do it again, or they head on to another area.

The Manta Ray that joined us decided to stay and do several rounds of this process with us. Where I was positioned was directly in the line of the path the ray took, and what happened during these fifteen or so minutes was the magic I had been looking for. For the Manta Ray to feel safe to swim up, our bodies have to rest with our legs up and behind us. They accomplish this by placing a pool noodle under your ankles, this allows the ray to safely swim up and circle without running into anyone's legs.

So here I am in the middle of the platform in the pathway for the circling majestic giant, and I'm beyond in awe as it swims under me - heart to heart. I could feel the huge heart this magical animal had and I was overwhelmed with love, joy, and feeling so much gratitude. At one point, my husband pops his head up and says to me, "Wow, that ray is really into you!!" I was like, and "I'm totally into them!" At one point, every time the Ray would circle up, it was so close to me it was bumping my chest. I felt this magnificent animal sharing its heart with me, and I was in pure awe. This was the moment I had been waiting for that only showed up once I let go.

Still, to this day, I sink into this memory, and I am filled with the joy of that moment, I almost feel transported back to that moment when I think of it.

Lesson: Letting go of our expectations and embracing the flow of life can lead to unexpected and enriching experiences.

Allowing ourselves to let go of our plans and go with the flow of life can lead to many wonderful and unexpected experiences. People often go into life with strong ideas and set plans, but they find that reality does not always go according to their plans. This can make us angry, let down, and feel like we are not in sync with the world around us. As soon as we let go of our tight grip on how we think things should go, we let life's spontaneity and unpredictability come in, which often comes with its own rewards and shocks.

Accepting the flow of life means letting go and trusting it. It means recognizing that we can not always control everything that happens in our lives and that going with the flow is sometimes better than going against it. This way of thinking does not mean being passive; instead, it means being able to change with the times and take advantage of the chances that come our way. When we let go of rigid standards, we can enjoy the present moment, pay more attention to our surroundings, and be more open to the lessons and joys each day brings.

This way of thinking also leads to a sense of peace and happiness. We lower the stress and anxiety of needing to be in charge when we do not hold on to specific outcomes. Life is good the way it is, not how we think it should be. By being open to the unexpected, we can find beauty and value in it, and the journey itself, not just the goal, can bring us joy. Every event, planned or unplanned, is seen as a chance to learn and grow. It encourages a mindset of gratitude and curiosity.

Letting go of our expectations and going with the flow of life is a great way to live a happier, less stressful life. It tells us to be adaptable, strong, and open to all the different options life offers us. This way of thinking can help us have a wider range of events that help us learn more about ourselves and the world around us. To remember that the best paths are not always the ones we planned and that life's surprises can teach us the most important things.

Chapter 21

A Preview Of The Future

After this magical night, I was at peace with going home. The Big Island once again showered her magic upon me and I knew inspiration would arise from this trip. The next morning, we took one last adventure and hiked the nearby Polol[1] Valley Beach. I had hiked here 5 years prior and wanted to take my family there before we left. We hiked the trail with Charlotte's daughters and had one last adventure down to the black sand beach and beautiful valley.

Once we were done, we headed back toward Hawi and stopped in Kohala to grab lunch. Turned out we were next door to Charlotte's office, so I messaged her. We chatted a bit through text, and then she said "oh, you need to go see the retreat center there, let me reach out to them." A few minutes later we found out we could stop by, so off we went.

We drove onto this property that was lush and tucked away from the busyness of the world. I was taken in by all the beauty this property had to offer. We connected with the contact, and he drove us around the property. Eventually, he took us to the spa and yoga studio, we walked into the gate to the area with these dwellings, and to my amazement, I was in the place I saw in my dream just a year and a half prior!

I looked out to an infinity pool with two welcoming mermaids. My husband was in front of me, with my son and Charlotte's daughters walking together in front of him. All I could think was, "THIS IS THE POOL FROM MY DREAM". Whoa, this was trippy and exciting and, well, another affirmation of why I was being nudged to trust the process and let go.

I immediately texted Charlotte and told her that she sent me to the place in my dream, she of course said, "Yep there's the magic of the Island!"

When I left, I was whirling with what was in my head. I had to soften up the need for things to make sense and trust in the process of what was to come, and what came from this is definitely way better than anything I could have dreamed up! This is the moment I'm really being asked to settle into trusting the divine has everything I need set up for me and that I can flow with it.

As with all my journeys and adventures, what I need to know unfolds later, in the moment, it's about being present, everything else unfolds just at the perfect time and moment I need it.

Reflection: Embracing change and uncertainty can open doors to new opportunities and a deeper understanding of our life's journey.

Accepting doubt and change is a big part of the path to growth and self-discovery. Life itself is always changing and growing, which means that we will always have to deal with change and instability. Sometimes, these things can be scary at first, but they can also help you grow as a person and lead to new chances you did not expect. When we learn to accept and even look forward to change, we leave our comfort zones behind and start a journey of learning and exploration.

We have to learn new skills, adapt, and rethink our views and perceptions when things change. It forces us to rethink our goals and values, which helps us learn more about what is important to us. On the other hand, uncertainty makes people stronger and more adaptable. It teaches us how to be flexible and creative when things go wrong in life. These events make us better people, which makes us better able to handle problems in the future with more confidence and knowledge.

Also, being open to change and doubt can make your life more interesting and full. It lets us experience new countries, ideas, and points of view, which helps us learn more about the world and our place in it. We are more likely to try new things, take risks, and follow our interests with an open mind. Having these experiences not only helps us grow as people, but they also make us happy and fulfilled.

To put it simply, accepting change and uncertainty means seeing the chance for growth in every situation. It is about realizing that life is not a straight line of predictable events. Instead, it is a winding road full of different situations that make us who we are. When we have an attitude that is open to change and opti-mistic about the unknown, we give ourselves the power to live a fuller life, seeing every moment as a chance to learn and grow. When we look at life this way, problems become opportunities to grow as people. Our journey is not just about the places we visit; it is also about the lessons and experiences we gain along the way.

Chapter 22

The Shift Begins

The year after our trip to Hawaii was filled with smaller journeys and very big transitions in my life. My son is now no longer a child, and the transition from mom of a young person to a young adult isn't always easy. As a mother, you want your child to go out into the world and find their way but that doesn't mean it's easy as you are going through it. A big part of my identity for 20 years was being his mom.

In full transparency, I struggled here, I had lots of trips and falls and it certainly didn't go as I had envisioned. See, that's the thing about manifesting, if I put the vision in a box I'm assured suffering. Although it was a harder road for me, it was the road I was meant to take. Ultimately, once we moved through the hard parts I was gifted another lesson, acceptance, and gratitude for what is.

I'm so grateful he took his life in his way, and I'm so proud of the man he is I know he is manifesting the life of his dreams, I trust that we both gained what we needed from the transition and I know we are better versions of ourselves because we challenged one another to grow.

With this transition came a need for me to lean into my faith in the divine and to allow myself to be supported and guided. I leaned into my self-care more and focused on my purpose and the work I'm in this life to experience. I was tremendously grateful for my soul sisters and the practices I had cultivated over the many years of my work in the holistic wellness field. Without all I do, I don't know if I'd be here now feeling the peace I do about all the change. With this change, it was a call from the divine to step up and into my purpose even more.

Every experience I have had led me here, step by step, to live my Authentic Life out loud.

So, I turned my focus to myself. I took more care of my body, mind, and spirit, and as I did, the messages and guidance of what to do next came through. I was already moving in the direction of what ultimately has now become my life and work but this focus put me in hyperdrive in a sense. I can see with more clarity and honor the guidance I'm receiving with more ease.

What came from shifting perspective and focus is without a doubt the absolute best thing I could have done for what came next was a dream come true!

Insight: Life transitions, though often challenging, can be powerful opportunities for self-reflection, growth, and redirection toward our true passions.

Transformations in life, whether planned or unplanned, often bring a mix of challenges and chances. Changes in work, personal relationships, moving, or big life events like marriage, having a child, or retirement are all examples of transitions. Even though they can be scary, they can also be a great way to learn more about yourself and grow. When things change, they push us out of our habits and comfort zones, forcing us to face new facts and rethink our goals and priorities. Even though this time of change may be full of worry, it is also a great time to learn more about ourselves and rethink what is important to us.

During times of change, we often have to look more closely at our lives and question the ways and decisions we are making right now. This process of thinking about ourselves can help us learn important things about our ideals, wants, and goals. It gives us a one-of-a-kind chance to change our lives so they align with who we are and what we love. For many people, big changes can be a wake-up call that makes them rethink what success and happiness mean. They can motivate us to get back into hobbies we have put on hold, learn new skills, or even start a new job that fits our values and makes us happier.

Going through changes in your life can also make you stronger and more flexible. We gain a better sense of who we are and more faith in our ability to handle whatever life throws at us as we learn to deal with change and the unknowns that come with it. These events teach us how important it is to be adaptable and accept that change is a normal part of life. They tell us that sometimes we need to leave the known and go into the unknown in order to grow.

In conclusion, life changes, even though they can be hard, are important ways to learn about yourself and grow as a person. These moments tell us to stop, think, and make choices about the way our lives are going. When we see these changes as chances, we can come out of them with a stronger sense of purpose and a new-found love for life. They are not just times of change; they are turning points that can change our paths and lead us to more real and satisfying experiences.

Chapter 23

Dream Big And
Receive Big Rewards

Next to Hawaii, I have dreamed of crossing the pod and taking a European trip. This seemed such a far chance, and I never really believed it was possible until I went to Hawaii the first time. The trip to Hawaii solidified an awareness in me that wasn't fully accessed before that magical trip. I believed anything was possible, and my whole mindset shifted from one of lack and fear to one of abundance and joy.

From 2016-2017, I traveled to so many places I never could have imagined Toronto, Hawaii, Sedona, The Texas Hill Country, Asheville, and Alaska. The year and a half of adventures were the seedlings to the life I'm now leading. A life filled with abundance, joy, adventure, and so much more. Without these adventures, I would never have been willing to take the biggest leap of faith yet.

On June 14, 2022, I made another commitment to my life adventures, and this one was a big one because it would take me overseas to Greece. I had so much resistance to taking this leap for so many years, and this was the day that spirit stirred in me and said, "Now is the time, dear one." I immediately took action and sought out the adventure I would take: a yoga retreat! That day, I booked the retreat and my flights, and when it was done, I was going to Europe, more specifically Greece.

I had many countries I dreamed of visiting throughout my life: Ireland, Italy, Spain, and more, but Greece would meet several bucket list items in one. I have a degree in Theater, and so much of the history of theater is in Greece. I also dove into the divine feminine work and connecting to the goddesses of all cultures, and finally, a yoga retreat to connect to my work and passion for helping others. With all of these connections, this was the perfect place for me to go.

This trip would be a solo trip and provided me with many things to consider regarding my travel plans and my uncertainty about navigating a country I have never been to. I spent the next several months preparing for this grand adventure and processing many thoughts and emotions. My husband has been the master planner of trips we have taken over the years, and I took action with the planning similar to how he had modeled preparation.

With each question or concern, I researched vlogs with guidance on where to go and how to travel safely. My travel would be ten days in the magical country of Greece and I had everything planned and ready to book intercountry travel. I had paused booking my additional intercountry travel until I was closer to my departure date, and I'm grateful I did because in early August my retreat was canceled.

Even though the retreat had been canceled, I knew I would be ok and I'd find a solution, so back to the retreat booking site, I would have to go. I already had my flight to take me to Athens, and I was grateful I had paused booking my intercountry travel because now I had flexibility. As a yoga teacher, being flexible isn't just about having a flexible body but, more importantly, about having a flexible mind. This practice was such a gift to me at this moment because I could allow things to change and shift without feeling the world was coming in on me.

I immediately began to search the retreat booking site and found several options, but was uncertain about the locations and travel between islands. I found myself spending a whole Sunday searching for a retreat and communicating with retreat facilitators, and finally, I landed on a new retreat. It was being held on the exact same dates as my previous retreat but on a different island. So now, instead of two locations in Greece, I would now visit three locations as I still felt called to visit Santorini, where the original retreat was being held, while I was there, and let me tell you, I know that was a divinely guided decision.

Once the retreat was booked, I began to evaluate my stays and adjusted everything. Instead of three days in Athens, I would stay one and then fly to Santorini for two days, finally to Andiparos by ferry, and finally back to Athens for my flight home. I was nervous and excited all in the same breath. The more I planned, the safer I felt to take this journey, and when the day came to leave, I was ready!

Takeaway: Dreaming big and taking actionable steps towards those dreams can turn them into reality, often exceeding our expectations.

The first step on a path to success and transformation is having big dreams. It means releasing ourselves from the limitations of uncertainty and fear to visualize our greatest goals and ambitions. But, without concrete efforts to convert them into reality, dreams are insufficient on their own. This journey from dream to reality calls for perseverance, preparation, and frequently a risk-taking mentality. We begin to see results when we divide our aspirations into doable objectives and diligently pursue them. Despite obstacles and disappointments along the way, this kind of trip is also quite fulfilling because it moves us one step closer to achieving our goals.

It also takes some bravery and resiliency to move toward our dreams. To pursue something important and meaningful, we have to be prepared to leave our comfort zones, face our anxieties, and deal with the uncertainty that accompanies this journey. This could entail learning new skills, looking for resources or mentors, or even altering our way of life. Although the journey is rarely clear-cut or simple, our difficulties frequently aid in our personal development. They impart important knowledge about tenacity, flexibility, and the value of being loyal to our goals.

Furthermore, we frequently discover that our dreams grow and change as we work toward them. A basic concept can potentially develop into something far bigger than we could have ever dreamed. This evolution represents our personal development and is a normal aspect of the journey. Our dreams change to reflect the new knowledge and experiences we gain about the world and ourselves. Frequently, the reality we construct surpasses our initial projections, resulting in an immensely gratifying feeling of accomplishment.

Simply put, having big aspirations and moving toward them with action is a dynamic and fulfilling process. It inspires us to see past our seeming boundaries, to welcome the possibilities of what may be, and to actively strive toward bringing those possibilities to pass. This trip is about who we become on the way, not just about reaching a destination. It is evidence of the strength of human ambition and the amazing capacity each of us has to mold our own lives and realize our aspirations.

Chapter 24

The Adventure Of A Lifetime

September 20, 2023, I headed to the airport and was off on the adventure I had only dreamed of for my whole life. There were two flights, one to Philadelphia and then overnight to Greece. I had scheduled myself to arrive early on the 21st to stay awake and power through to explore. The flight arrived on time at 9 AM, I made it! Each hotel I had booked offered the option of pre-booking travel to and from the airport or ferry, and I'm grateful I did this because it brought so much ease to my experience. I get through customs and out to find my transport to find many drivers with names on cards. I searched through the crowd of drivers and finally found mine.

We headed off to my hotel in the heart of Athens, and I was consumed with the visions I was taking in. As soon as I landed, I felt this sense of belonging, like I had been here before, and I knew at that moment I would have a perfectly safe and joyful experience. As we drove into the city, I was in awe of the whole environment, from the topography to the buildings and architecture.

As we found our way to the city's heart I began to see some of the ancient ruins and couldn't wait to get out and put my feet on the earth and explore. My hotel was within steps of everything I wanted to visit and see, and I was ready to get out and see it all. I checked into my quaint hotel in a square with garden restaurants and shops just doors away. I settled in my room and needed nourishment, so I washed up a bit and headed out for breakfast, a coffee and to find my way to the Acropolis.

In the square, I found a place to eat breakfast and have a coffee, one of the best meals I think I've ever had. It was so simple, but the food was fresh and tasted so flavorful. I sat and observed the regulars having their morning communion with each other and soaked in the simplicity of this moment. It was such a perfect way to begin my first day in Greece.

Once I was done, I began to walk aimlessly toward The Acropolis. I generally had an idea of how to get there, but I was in no hurry, I just wanted to be in the moment. I found shops and small ruins within the city streets, observed the architecture and the locals and visitors moving through their day. Until I came to a wide street and decided which direction to turn. I turned to the right as I saw many people moving in that direction, and as soon as I did I came around a tree, and there it was the Acropolis and the Parthenon.

Lesson: Solo travel and exploring new cultures can be deeply empowering, offering invaluable lessons in independence, resilience, and open-mindedness.

Solo travel is more than just sightseeing; it is a trip to learn more about yourself and gain confidence.

When you go on a trip alone, you leave your safety zone and see the world however you choose. This experience teaches you a lot about independence as you get around in new places, solve problems, and make choices without asking anyone else for help. Every problem you solve and contact you make go well, no matter how small, and boosts your confidence and sense of independence. Solo travel also makes you more aware and present, letting you be more in touch with your thoughts and feelings as well as your surroundings.

As a solo traveler, you can also work on being strong and flexible by experiencing new countries. It takes flexibility and an open mind to immerse yourself in places you do not know fully and whose languages, cultures, and social norms are different from your own. It can be confusing at first, but it also helps you see things in a new way and challenges your biases and preconceived ideas. Getting involved with people from different countries helps you understand the world better and develops empathy and respect for differences. It also makes you feel like a global citizen by telling you that even though we come from different places, we all have the same hopes and experiences.

Also, traveling by yourself is a great way to think about yourself and observe. When you get away from the daily stresses and routines, you have time to think about the big things in life, your goals and values, and the path you want your life to take. Traveling by yourself can give you deep experiences and new ideas that can help you grow and change as a person. The peaceful times to think, the beautiful sunsets in a foreign country, and the talks with strangers that turn into friends are the things that you will remember long after the trip is over.

Traveling alone and learning about other cultures are not just about the physical trip; they are also about the journey of the mind and spirit. They show kids how to be independent, strong, and open-minded, and they teach them the joy of finding out about new things. Solo travel can be very empowering and life-changing, whether it is a short trip to a nearby city for the weekend or a long trip across countries over several months. It not only shows you the world, but also new sides of yourself. It often gives you a new sense of purpose and a greater understanding of how different people's lives are.

Chapter 25

Feeling The Power
Of The Ancient Land

As I began to hike my way up to the Parthenon, there was so much to see, including relics of the Theater of Dionysus. There were many relics and points to read and explore the ruins, and I was taking it all in. As a theater major, this was feeding a part of my soul that I had resting quietly dormant for many years as I was no longer immersed in the theater. It brought me back to memories of my years in high school and college and the magic of the theater. It reminded me of where I came from and how much I had grown.

After taking in all this magic, I moved on and climbed higher and higher to the entry to the many ancient buildings that rest atop The Acropolis. As I walked through the entry, I could feel so many things, emotions, connections, and ultimately, the power of the land and all it held. I was someplace I had only ever dreamed of, and I couldn't believe it was real for a moment. I remember sending a message to my goddess soul sisters because I could feel the presence of the Goddess Athena. She was everywhere in this city, but her temple was here.

The time I spent exploring The Acropolis was the first time in my life that I could say I needed to be pinched because it was so surreal. It was such a dream come true to be here, and I was filled with so much gratitude. After my time at the Acropolis, I headed back to my hotel for a rest as I had another adventure to experience in the evening.

Later that afternoon, I got ready and headed out for dinner and then off to my motorized bicycle tour. I had dinner, another amazing meal, and then walked over to meet the tour group. When I arrived I was given a bike to get used to riding as I had never been on a motorized bicycle. We waited for the rest of our group to arrive, only to find they never came, so my tour would be solo. My guide was so kind, and we had such a lovely time together as we rode all over the city to see every site I planned to see over three days but now only had one day. This was the best way to see the city and all its historical places. At one point, the guide looked at me and said "You are making me feel so relaxed. Normally, I feel pressure when on these tours." I, of course said, "Well, that's what I'm here for – a relaxed adventure!" Once we returned, it was dark, and I wasn't exactly sure how to get back to my hotel, so she gave me a suggestion of how to get back, and off I went.

I arrived back at my hotel. I got ready for bed and then needed to plug in my phone and in perfect order, I blew the circuit and the electricity went out on the whole floor of my hotel! I had to find the attendant, and he feverishly sought to reset the circuit, luckily, within a short bit of time, the lights were on again, and I headed off to bed. My flight to Santorini was the next day, and I had to be up and ready quite early.

The next morning I came down to find the same driver from the day before was there to take me back to the airport. When I booked my first retreat, the facilitator had sent out some notes about the customs in Greece, and one of the things they shared was that if a local offers to pay for something, you should say thank you and accept the kindness, otherwise, they may be offended. I had not encountered this as of yet, but sure enough, I did that morning. As we were leaving, I thought I'd have time to grab a coffee, but I did not. When we got to the car, I saw a small coffee stand open and asked if I could grab a cup of coffee before we left. The driver walked over with me, and once I ordered, she paid for the coffee and then bought me a treat they had at the stand. I, of course, said thank you and accepted the kindness.

Reflection: Connecting with historical and cultural landmarks can provide a profound sense of belonging and a deeper connection to the human experience.

Getting to know historical and cultural sites is a rewarding experience that goes beyond just looking at them. These landmarks are more than just buildings or artifacts; they are living links to our past that hold the stories, battles, and victories of those who lived before us. When you visit these places, you feel like you are a part of a bigger human story. It lets us stand where important historical events happened, touch walls that have been there for hundreds of years, and look at art that has moved people for generations. When we think about how much time has passed and how different cultures are linked, this link can make us feel very emotional.

These sites also give us a powerful look at what it means to be human. They tell us of the many cultures in the world and the history we all share. We can put ourselves in the shoes of people from different times and places when we visit historic sites, ruins, or cities. We learn more about their lives, views, and traditions, which helps us understand humanity and its different forms. This exploration makes us realize how small our lives are in the grand plan of things and how quickly they can end.

Also, seeing these sites often makes people feel amazed and awed. The grandeur of a medieval cathedral, the mystery of ancient ruins, or the beauty of a painting from hundreds of years ago can all stir the soul and spark the mind. They inspire us and make us think about the amazing things people have done with their creativity and cleverness. In today's fast-paced world, where many things are temporary and digital, these real reminders of the past give us a sense of stability and permanence.

Connecting with historical and cultural landmarks is a highly meaningful experience that helps us understand life's journey. It helps people feel like they are part of a bigger story and helps them appreciate how different and rich human society is. The ties between people remind us of our ancestors and their marks on the world. They also make us consider the marks we will leave for future generations. Thinking about history and culture is not just a mental practice; it is also a deeply personal experience that helps us learn more about who we are and where we come from.

Chapter 26

Magical Santorini

I arrived at the airport, moved through the baggage checkpoint, and headed down to my gate. This flight was very quick and on a smaller plane than I was used to. I had to take a bus to get to the plane, and we walked up mobile stairs to board the plane, this was a first for me. Once on the plane, it was a quick 45 minutes, and we were in Santorini. I exited, grabbed my luggage, and then found my driver.

The hotel I chose in Santorini was outside of the larger towns, and I chose it because it included transport to the airport, ferry, and the towns. I figured it was sounder to pay a little more and stay somewhere that included my transportation; this was for sure the best plan. Once I checked in, I hung out at the pool for a short while and then was off on the Sunset catamaran tour I had booked.

The tour was so much fun. I met a family from Texas, and we had a grand time enjoying the sights, the wine, and the food that was prepared on board. This would be the first experience I would have with the Aegean Sea, seeing the island from the sea was inspiring and breathtaking. I felt so much joy here with the company and the connection to the land and sea. Toward the end of the tour, just before the sunset, we anchored off to eat dinner, watch and sunset, and swim in the water.

The water was so clear you could see to the bottom, the clarity reminded me of the springs in Florida. The temperature of the water also reminded me of the springs, as it was quite cold, but I didn't care I was still enjoying this moment fully. Once the sunset we headed back into the port and on back to our hotels. My sleep that night was so good as I was very tired from the jet lag and the abundance of adventure!

The next day, I found my way to both Fira, the capital of Santorini, and Oia, the most popular town seen in movies. In the morning I explored Fira, went shopping and found the bracelet I still wear today, and had a magical lunch looking out over the Sea. I stepped into the church and felt the presence of the divine in this dwelling and every stretch of land my feet have stepped upon.

I took the afternoon to relax and enjoy the poolside at my hotel. The air was crisp, and the pool was cold, so I chose just to take in some sun and rest. For dinner, I took the transport to Oia and found a magical spot for dinner. Usually, Oia is the best place for the Sunset this particular night, the sky was overcast, and there would be no sunset – but that would not deter me. The dinner I had that night was high above the sea, and I met a lovely woman visiting with her husband from France. She was American and was originally from Florida. We had a lovely chat and enjoyed the magical meal. Everywhere I went, I found lovely souls to talk with, and I never felt alone, even when I was on my own completely. The dinner concluded with a most magical pistachio dessert and donkeys walking back up the steps of this most famous town.

After dinner, I found a few more shops to stop in and headed off to the meeting point for our trip back to the hotel. Once we returned, I touched base with my husband and then organized my things as the next day, I'd be off to my retreat on the ferry.

Insight: Embracing spontaneity and the beauty of the moment can lead to some of life's most memorable and joyful experiences.

A way of thinking that can change the way we live our lives is to embrace chance and the beauty of the present moment. We often spend much time planning every part of our lives, from short-term goals to daily tasks. Even though it is important to plan, being too rigid with our plans can cause us to miss out on the joys and wonders that life has to offer. Being spontaneous means being open to the unexpected, taking advantage of last-minute chances, and enjoying the present moment. This way of looking at life makes us more open to new experiences and flexible, which often leads to some of the most memorable and meaningful times of our lives.

Giving up all of your goals and responsibilities does not mean you are living spontaneously. Instead, it means being open to unplanned experiences and savoring every moment. It is about finding a balance between our planned activities and the fact that life is not always what we expect it to be. You might try a new place on a whim, walk along a different path, or even book a trip on the spur of the moment. In these times of spontaneity, we often have happy experiences that would not have happened if we stuck to a strict plan. In a way, they tell us that life is an adventure with many unknown turns and possibilities.

Taking in the beauty of the present moment also teaches us to value life as it happens. As we live in a world where we always look ahead or back, being spontaneous helps us stay in the present. It teaches us to treasure the short, sweet times that make life worth living. These times can be as easy as deciding on the spot to talk to a stranger, spend the night with friends without planning to, or watch the sunrise. Even though these things may not seem important, they can have a big effect on our happiness and sense of satisfaction.

Being open to the unexpected and the beauty of the present is a big part of living your best life. At the same time, we know we can not control everything, but we can choose to live our lives in an open, active, and present way. This way of thinking not only leads to fun and memorable events but it also makes you value the beauty and surprises that come up out of nowhere in life even more. It makes us remember that the best moments are not always the ones we planned and that the trip, not just the destination, is often where the real joy is.

Chapter 27

The Goddess Within

The ferry ride to Paros was an adventure and a time to rest up, for the next five days were sure to be a deep dive to connect with my authentic self and soul. As I shared before, this wasn't the first retreat I had chosen, and I now understand that this was the retreat that chose me. What I needed to do here was much more than just pause in a beautiful place, it was an opportunity to stir my soul and awaken the next level of my purpose and vision for my life and my work in this world.

As we arrived on the island, I had to find the only transportation I had not previously scheduled. I found myself turned around and dragging my suitcase over a rocky cobble sidewalk, feeling for the first time since I had arrived a bit out of sorts. Suddenly, I heard in my head turn around, so being a cultivator of my intuition, I listened, and sure enough, just to the opposite side of the dock was a bus that would take me to the next smaller short ferry I needed to take to get to Andiparos.

Once off the ferry, I had to walk the short distance to the hotel where the retreat would take place, once again walking along a cobbled sidewalk, it felt like a comedic movie scene dragging the suitcase and seeing the final destination but having to muddle through for the moment. Finally, I arrived and met the retreat facilitator. She took me directly to my room because the first event was starting in less than 45 minutes.

When booking the first retreat, I had chosen a private room, but when I had scheduled the new retreat, the only available room was a shared suite and room. Upon arrival, I met my suitemate and then my roommate. In quite a hurried state, I settled my things and then needed to pause to regroup as I was a bit frazzled. Once I grounded myself, I was ready to step into this week with purpose.

The retreat was called The Goddess Within, and little did I know what would come from this experience but it was life-changing. Each day, we met for yoga, self-exploration, and connecting to the deep levels of ourselves. I had been doing this work for quite some time and felt much of what we were doing was just an opportunity for me to sink in a little more and open my heart. As a guide for others, I do this work daily through sharing my stories, listening to another's story, and finding the connections to everything in my life that is being weaved for my greatest good by the divine.

As I listened and shared with this group of women, the illumination of the art of vulnerability and the gift of working in a circle with others was clearly what I was here for. To invite myself to feel these deep connections with a community that lives halfway across the world from me, but we are experiencing the same kinds of things. When we are isolated in our small piece of the world, it can be easy to let very small things take over our lives. This is the great gift of the self-love journey to recognize yourself in another person, to realize we are all here to help each other rise and step more fully into remembering who we really are.

The adventure we took over the retreat included work, but we also found time for rest and play. Being a Florida girl, I love to be in the water, specifically the Gulf Coast of Florida. One of the days, we had an option to participate in a boat tour, and I was, of course, up for that adventure. We began the day with yoga, meditation, and sacred circle time, and then a small group of us headed off on the boat. We were taken to several places to swim and explore, and I was immersed in every moment of this exploration.

The water was still as clear as could be, and I was ready to be in there swimming. As soon as we anchored off, we ate lunch, and then it was time to play! We swam and played and enjoyed the sun and the sea. We then moved off to our next destination, where we could cliff jump and swim into the water caves, I was going to do it all. As soon as we anchored off, I asked the captain if we were good, and he said, "Yes." I ripped off my shirt and dove in the water to the sounds of everyone yelling, "No, no, wait!" but I was already in the water. I swam over to the rocky edge and began to climb; eventually, I had to work my way to the edge and was ready to jump.

As I stood here at the edge of the cliff, I was reflecting on what happened the last time I jumped from a cliff and how that jump was a leaping-off point to break the foundation and create a whole new life. It felt kind of like a full-circle moment. I stood there looking down at the water, feeling nervous and still knowing I would be going for it. I heard all the women cheering me on and watching from the boat in excitement, and then I leaped, I hit the water and no pain, just exhilaration!

Within moments, the others begin to jump in the water and swim over to join me in the water cave. I had made jokes with them that I was a mermaid, and so as I swam into the cave, I began to sing a tone. A few other women who had joined me paused a bit before entering. I encouraged them and we all swam in the cave and laughed and sang. We spent a little more time here, then headed off to two stopping points where we could swim to a shore and just take it all in. That's what I did, I soaked up every moment because I wanted it to become part of me.

This practice of being in the moment and taking it all in is one I love about life. I have to actively work for it in other parts of my life, but in these moments, I'm all in! Once we returned to the hotel, a good rest was in store before our evening sessions. This was one of those days that will never be forgotten; it's one with me, and I am so grateful for the purity of it all and how it makes me feel when I reflect upon it.

As I reflect upon this whole week, there were so many moments I soaked up: lunch with my newfound friends, shopping excursions, the hike to see the sunset, our nightly group dinners, and the joy of every moment. As we came to the end of the retreat I was filled with many great awarenesses and new memories and friends to hold close to my heart. The last night, in particular, was where I felt the whole journey to Greece came to be understood.

Takeaway: Retreats and immersive experiences can provide the space and perspective needed for deep introspection and renewed self-awareness.

Immersive events and retreats are great places to really think about yourself and learn more about yourself. We can think about our lives, thoughts, and feelings without the normal pressures or distractions when we take a break from our daily routines and surroundings. These events usually happen in places that help people relax and think, like nature, peaceful retreat centers, or places with lots of history and culture. The mind can calm down in these places, which lets us go deeper into our inner world. This change of scenery not only takes our minds off of our daily lives but it also represents a shift in our emotions and minds, making it possible for us to explore ourselves in new and changing ways.

A lot of the time, skilled facilitators lead these kinds of events. They do things like yoga, meditation, workshops, and group talks to give structure and support. These activities help us concentrate better, become more aware, and find new thinking methods. When you go on a retreat or an immersive experience with other people going through similar things, you can share your thoughts and get help from each other. Hearing different stories and points of view can teach us new things and make us feel better by letting us know that we are not the only ones going through hard times or trying to reach their goals. This sense of belonging and having been through the same thing can be reassuring and powerful.

Also, the time spent thinking about yourself in these places can lead to big insights and a renewed sense of self-awareness. When we get away from the stress and noise of everyday life, we can hear our inner selves and get in touch with who we really are. This process can help us get clear on our ideals, our goals, and the changes we might want to make in our lives. When we have these kinds of experiences, we often learn things that make us want to make changes in our personal or work lives that are more in line with who we really are.

Finally, I want to say that retreats and other immersive events are great ways to learn more about yourself and grow as a person. They give people a place to get away from the stresses of everyday life and think, learn, and relax. These events can be turning points in our lives, giving us clarity, inspiration, and a fresh relationship with who we are. The time we spend reflecting and discovering ourselves, whether it is on a weekend retreat or a longer, more intense experience, can have a lasting effect, giving us the perspective and tools we need to live a more meaningful and fulfilling life.

Chapter 28

Goddess Realized

I have actively been on the journey of self-exploration, healing, and growth for 20 years now. I have a very intentional scope I have chosen to look at my life through, and I feel it has helped me to find my authentic self. The lens I see my life, in general, is fueled by love. That being said, I didn't know that I really knew how to love myself fully until these last few years—the time I spent in Greece brought me to a whole new level of love.

For the 20 years before my trip to Greece, I was so focused on being a provider that I couldn't see past the ego at times. I had so much I was "worried" about that I would find myself spinning out and having to reset with yoga, meditation, and other practices constantly. I constantly was working with the tools I taught to be the best version of myself, but I'm human and have times I fall and need those tools to help me. I never claimed to be perfect, but I did my best every day to grow and heal so I could be the best version of me I could be.

The summer before my trip, the dynamic in our home changed, and the driving force that had me so focused on providing changed. Now was the time to choose how I wanted to move forward, and this time in Greece changed me forever. I found a part of myself that had been covered up for years by this persona of "the provider," and it was time to shed this illusion.

On the closing night of our retreat, I was asked to lead our group in chanting, which I do as part of my sound healing work, and I said yes. As I led the group to chant together, I was filled with the presence of the divine, I was light and love and peace all in one breath. By the end of the chant, I was in tears because I felt the pure love of the divine moving through me. That night, the photographer took a candid shot of me while I was meditating. I did not know this until she reached out to me the weekend after I had returned home and asked if she could share the picture she took of me and sent me the image.

When I looked at this photo, I saw my true, authentic self, and she was beautiful. She was me, and for the first time in my life, I looked upon a photo of myself and saw no flaws, I only saw the love that I am. This time I was in Greece was an opening that couldn't have been experienced in any other way and it has been a key to open me up and truly and move me forward further upon my Authentic Life Journey.

Reflection: Moments of deep connection with the divine can be transformative, revealing our innermost beauty, strength, and purpose.

Having a moment of real connection with God is a powerful experience that can change our lives. People often call these times "transcendent awakenings" or "spiritual moments." They make us feel like we are one with the world and help us understand our place in it better. These kinds of links can happen in many places, like when we are meditating, in nature, or doing religious practices, or even just when we suddenly feel calm and clear. These events go beyond the physical world and touch the core of who we are, showing us our true beauty, strength, and purpose.

These divine relationships often help us learn things about ourselves and our lives that change everything. Because they can bring out our inner wants, fears, and truths, they can help us see ourselves more clearly and honestly. This greater clarity can give us a deeper sense of direction and purpose, which can be very empowering. It helps us live in a way that is more true to who we are and what we believe in. In addition, these times can give us a sense of inner peace and strength, allowing us to handle life's challenges with grace and bravery.

Also, connecting with the divine often makes people feel more linked and empathetic with others. A sense of universal unity grows when we see the divine in ourselves and others. As we become more aware of how all living things are linked, we can treat each other with more kindness and understanding. Because we feel responsible and love people and the land, it can motivate us to make the world a better place.

In the end, having a deep relationship with the divine opens the door to a lot of personal growth and enlightenment. They give us glimpses into the vastness of life and show us the beauty and promise that are inside us. These events tell us that there is more to life than meets the eye. They push us to dig deeper into our spirituality and live in a way that respects our deepest truths. Accepting these links can help us live a more meaningful, happy, and connected life with the world around us.

Chapter 29

New Inspirations to Expand the Heart, Mind, and Soul

Insight: Continued self-growth and exploration pave the way for new inspirations and opportunities, keeping us aligned with our evolving life's journey.

Continual introspection and self-improvement are essential to remaining in step with our changing life path. Our needs, wants, and objectives all change as we develop and mature. We can remain aware of these shifts and make sure we are heading in the right way by continuing our journey of self-discovery. This process entails periodically assessing our lives, thinking back on our past encounters, and remaining receptive to discovering new things about ourselves and the society we live in. By doing this, we can change and grow in genuine and satisfying ways.

Furthermore, on this path of self-improvement, we frequently discover fresh possibilities and sources of inspiration that we may not have previously considered. We become more open to a wider choice of options as we develop and learn. We may become aware of previously undiscovered passions or skills, which inspire us to seek new interests, occupations, or romantic endeavors. Every new encounter and bit of information broadens our viewpoint and deepens our awareness of who we are, enabling us to perceive possibilities where there formerly were only barriers.

Furthermore, ongoing introspection and development support our sense of direction and drive. It is simple to let our routines make us stale or complacent, but by actively searching out new experiences, we maintain our lives interesting and dynamic. We remain energized and enthusiastic about the future because we live a proactive lifestyle and acknowledge that there is always more to discover, do, and experience. It also aids in our ability to adjust to the inevitable ups and downs of life, seeing them as chances for continued development rather than obstacles.

Upon my return from Greece, I had a fire within me and a clarity of purpose that I was ready to create. The next months would include dreaming, creating, and finding solutions to help me get to the next great leap of faith. A leap I was willing to take and knew that the divine was there to support me. When we can open to our heart's purpose and truly take action on the nudges and inspirations, that's when life begins to feel more abundant and beautiful.

It's been a year since I was nudged to go and see what the world had in store for me, and I'm currently creating all the new things I'm here to create. I have been actively opening myself up to doing things that feel scary and setting aside time to write, create, and envision what will be manifested sooner than I know.

It took me a long time to trust in the process, and there are days I'm still working my way to trusting it all the time, but I'm closer today than was, and I know that as long as I continue to walk this path more will be revealed in perfect time and order. I don't know how I'll get to the next right step, but I don't have to. I just have to wake up every day and ask the divine, what do you want to create through me today? Then, I have to listen and take action.

My journeys over these last seven years have taught me so many lessons. Some of the lessons are in support of the tools I teach. Others are simply the lessons I needed to experience to open up to my divine loving self and to live her out loud without fear or concern, for I am a magical spark of the divine, and I have the gift to be the light for my life and in support of others. Every adventure, journey, or experience is my teacher, and it's up to me to see the magic in it all. I am forever grateful for my life and for every messy and beautiful experience that it has offered me.

I leave you here knowing this is not the end, actually, it's just the beginning! Friends, I invite you to seek out the magic in life, to see where the divine is showing up, and to gaze upon everything as an opportunity and, ultimately, a gift. For that is what this life is — a gift.

With Infinite Love & Gratitude
Ramona

ACKNOWLEGMENTS

As I embark on this transformative journey through the pages of my book, I am filled with immense gratitude for each of you who has chosen to accompany me on this path. Your presence is a cherished gift, and I am honored to share my experiences and insights with you.

A heartfelt thank you extends to my husband, Steve, whose unwavering belief in my dreams has provided the fertile ground for creating this work. His grounded and safe space has been my refuge during the creative process, and I am blessed to have him by my side.

To Bryce and Lily, my son and daughter-in-law, your excitement for my endeavors and steadfast support have been integral to bringing my dream business and life to fruition. I am deeply grateful for your encouragement and enthusiasm.

I also want to express my appreciation to the inspiring individuals who have played pivotal roles in shaping the practitioner and friend I am today. Paige, Susan, Jody, Erin, and Charlotte, your influence and presence in my life have been profound, and I am thankful for the inspiration you have provided as part of this book and my life as a whole. I'd like to offer a special thanks to Donna for allowing me to stay at her beach retreat to write many of the pages of this book.

To my extended family, friends, and clients, your contribution to my growth and the discovery of my authentic voice has been invaluable. Each life experience shared with you has been a stepping stone toward becoming the holistic practitioner I am today.

A special acknowledgment goes to my sister, Sarah, who has seen me, challenged me to grow, and encouraged me to claim my greatness. Our soul-stirring conversations have solidified my path as a guide, empowering others to find and live their authentic lives out loud.

In gratitude and love,
Ramona Crabtree-Falkner

Made in the USA
Las Vegas, NV
25 January 2024

84894516R00083